TRUSTEE HANDBOOK

Fifth Edition

National Association of Independent Schools

18 Tremont Street, Boston, Massachusetts 02108

ISBN 0-934338-54-X

The Authors

First edition, 1964; second edition, 1970; third edition, 1974

Francis Parkman, A.B., A.M., Ph.D. Harvard University, L.H.D. (hon.) Tufts University, served as headmaster of Saint Mark's School (Mass.) from 1930 to 1942 and, following military service, as executive officer of the National Council of Independent Schools from 1948 to 1962. In April 1962, when the National Council merged with the Independent Schools Education Board to create NAIS, Dr. Parkman was appointed the first president of the new organization and directed its affairs until his retirement, in September 1963. In retirement, Dr. Parkman has continued his service to independent education as an adviser to NAIS and consultant to its member schools.

E. Laurence Springer, A.B. Princeton University, M.A. University of Buffalo, Litt.D. (hon.) Princeton University, served on the governing board of the National Council of Independent Schools, was involved in the affairs of the Independent Schools Education Board, and was chairman of the committee that planned the merger of the two organizations, in 1962. He was headmaster of The Pingry School (N.J.) from 1936 until his early retirement, in 1961, when he established an office as educational consultant in La Jolla, California, serving as an adviser to independent school trustees and heads.

Fourth edition, 1980, and fifth edition, 1984

Eric W. Johnson, A.B. Harvard University, M.A.T. Harvard Graduate School of Education. Mr. Johnson's career as teacher and administrator in independent schools spans 36 years, 25 of which were spent at Germantown Friends School (Pa.), where he taught English, history, and sex education and served, at various times, as head of the junior high school, director of development, coordinator of public relations, and vice principal. For four years (1948-1952) he was head of Friends' Central School (Pa.). Mr. Johnson is well known in the school world — public as well as independent — as the author of textbooks and workshops in English, literature, and motivation as well as books on teaching and sex education. He is author of 31 books, including *Teaching School: Points Picked Up* and *Evaluating the Performance of Trustees and School Heads,* which NAIS published in 1979 and 1983, respectively. Mr. Johnson is now clerk of the school committee (chairman of the board of trustees) of Germantown Friends School, a position to which he was named in 1978 shortly after leaving daily teaching to devote full time to writing and to advising schools.

Contents

4. The Board and the Head / **38**

5. Selecting a New Head and Getting Started / **58**

6. A Postscript / **68**

Preface

This handbook presents generally accepted principles of sound practice for the governance and administration of independent schools. Although addressed primarily to trustees, who bear the ultimate legal responsibility, it is equally concerned with the responsibilities of the school head for the educational leadership and management of the school and with the quality of the working relationship between board and head, upon which the success of the school depends.

The key importance of this relationship — ideally, a partnership of mutual endeavor and trust — has been the central theme of the *Trustee Handbook* since it was first published, in 1964. It deserves even greater emphasis in today's climate, which finds independent schools contending with financial pressures and challenges that make the need for sure hands at the helm, and for communication and understanding between boards and heads, essential. We hope the handbook will serve both trustees and heads as a resource and basis for assuring the effective leadership of their schools.

We are pleased that Eric Johnson agreed to prepare the fourth edition and this fifth edition of the handbook. We believe the original authors, Francis Parkman and E. Laurence Springer, will again be pleased with the fruits of his efforts. Although this edition reflects changes in the responsibilities and expectations of boards and heads and recognizes new concerns, the substance, flavor, and much of Parkman's and Springer's text have been retained. As Mr. Johnson notes, the basic principles expounded by his distinguished predecessors will remain valid as long as there are independent schools to be governed.

We are very much in debt, also, to the many trustees and heads whose comments and editorial suggestions were reflected in the 1980 edition, and most particularly to the members of the NAIS Trustee Committee.

John C. Esty, Jr.
President, NAIS

1.

Boards of Trustees

The primary responsibility of the board of trustees of an independent school is to see to it that the institution operates in the best interests of its students, teachers, and parents. It has a larger and more continuing responsibility, too, which is reflected in the word "trustee," for a school should be held in trust.

The trustees are custodians of the integrity of the institution, of its standing and reputation built by the founders and those who have labored over the years. Trustees hold in trust the school's future as well as its present. Their collective judgment affects it as an instrument of service to constituents who are to come and to society as a whole, of which all independent schools are a part. School heads come, have their influence, and go. Only the trustees, as a body, represent continuity and permanent responsibility.

As nonprofit, tax-exempt institutions, independent schools must serve, each in its own way, the public welfare. They cannot be justified if their primary function is to provide more strength and privilege to the already strong and privileged. They must teach that good education is a loan to be repaid by the gift of self.

Because independent schools are privately managed, they can operate in large measure independently of state and federal prescriptions. Thus they are free to experiment by trying out new ways and holding firm to old ways that may not now be the fashion, and they may stand firm for moral and spiritual values. Their freedom obligates them to serve the common welfare as a part of the vast enterprise of education in the United States. Governing boards must see to it that the schools they hold in trust share with others their experience and professional skill in developing educational thought and practice in their communities and in the nation.

Division of responsibilities: board and head

The school will do its work best if board and head understand and accept a basic division of responsibilities. The board sets the purpose and the policies of the school; the head operates the school so as to achieve the purpose and carry out the policies. The board appoints the head and delegates to the head responsibility for operating the school. Board members must never interfere or get involved in operations unless the head specially invites them to do so. Heads should do their best to see that their boards have all the information they need to carry out their functions, develop sound policies, and judge accurately how well those policies are being carried out.

Trustees should not be tempted to think of school heads as people who merely carry out the decisions of others. Heads who are worth their salt see themselves as educational leaders. They are bound to have, and their boards should rightly expect them to have, plenty of ideas about school policies and plans for their boards to consider.

Although a major leader of the school, a sort of prime minister or prime mover, the head must never forget that the board is boss. Defining and approving objectives and policies is a process that works best when it involves deep and frequent communication between head and board. As this process goes on, the board should allow the administration to conduct its affairs within the framework of established policies and support it in every way possible while at the same time assessing its performance. This division of responsibility for a common endeavor is the fundamental rule for successful functioning of the board and for successful relations with the head.

Board composition and responsibilities

Let us now turn to some other principles that have emerged from the experience of many thriving schools, while remembering that the very independence of independent schools means that they operate successfully in many different ways and that each is unique. No board or head should be distressed if the structure of governance of the school differs from the structures suggested here. If the school works well, let it work. If there are problems, frictions, weaknesses, frustrations, or stubborn inadequacies, the suggestions that follow here may help.

Size of board. Governing boards vary greatly in size, ranging from 10 to 50, and no magic number should be prescribed. Most boards consist of 15 to 20 members. A large board can more easily represent the various constituencies of the school and provide a greater pool of available and diversified talent. At the same time, having a large board increases the danger of dispersed energy and responsibility and diluted feelings of involvement by individual members. A larger board is harder to manage and coordinate.

Diversity of talent. More important than the size of the board are the dedication, competence, and stature of its members. Among the many attempts to give pithy, alliterative definitions of the ideal trustee, one version has it that "affluence, influence, and interest" are what is needed. Another says that a trustee should be "dynamic, diligent, and decisive," and a ready "contributor of care, cash, comfort, and counsel." A third has it that a useful trustee should contribute at least two of the following three: wealth, work, and wisdom. While in all of them there is a reference to ability to give money (and a wealthy and generous trustee is a blessing), it would be unfortunate if able and interested men and women of modest means were deterred from, or not considered suitable for, serving by the expectation that a trustee must be able to give large sums of money as well as time and thought.

All sources of talent and experience should be systematically explored. The nominating committee of the board, advised by the chairman and the head of the school, should have in mind the kinds of people needed to fill vacancies, maintain lists, and cultivate prospects so that as vacancies occur needed talents may be added to the board. Choosing board members primarily from one profession or walk of life, or from those who can bring only limited experience to handling the school's affairs, should be avoided. A board should reflect strength, vision, experience, a blending of educational, managerial, investment, business, and legal talents, and knowledge of the surrounding community as required. Such diversity permits a board to make its maximum contribution to school administration.

There are several sorts of imbalance to which some boards tend and thus fail to achieve the best mix of talent and experience. One is to have mostly business people on the board, with perhaps a lawyer or two to provide counsel. Without doubt, business talents, and the resources that go with them, are essential to the proper and useful functioning of boards. Quite obviously, however, a school is not a business (even though some important aspects of its operation are) but a human endeavor. Its object is not profit, except the profit of society. The object is the fullest possible development of the talents of human beings so that they may be useful, productive members of society.

Another imbalance arises from the understandable but naive belief that, since a school is an educational institution, education is what trustees should know best, and that the board should therefore be composed predominantly of teachers and school people. Such boards do not serve well in the fullest sense. The board should remember that the head and the faculty are the main educators in the school. They are professionally qualified, and what they most need is not more professional educational judgment but, rather, the lay judgment and skills and support for their work that can come from men and women of different talents: commerce, finance, law, politics, community organization, public communication, and dealing with property and buildings – their construction, maintenance, acquisition, and disposition.

Yet another form of imbalance exists in not reflecting on the board the diversity already represented in the school at large or in not having the board take the lead in introducing greater diversity into the school community. Women and minority trustees – and not necessarily those from traditional sources – come particularly to mind in this connection. Schools that pursue and achieve minority representation on the board often find the added perspectives of minorities invaluable, and they enjoy greater credibility and rapport with minority agencies and communities from whom they seek prospective minority families.

Essential qualifications for trustees

Talent is one thing, its proper use is another. In order to serve usefully on a board of trustees, a candidate should be able to answer yes to the following questions or have a confident yes said by the nominating committee.

• Are the candidate's views on life and education generally congenial with the stated fundamental goals and purposes of the school, and can this person keep the ultimate purposes of the school in mind whenever decisions are to be made? Can he or she keep a sense of perspective?

• Does the candidate have talents, abilities, and experience that the school needs on its governing board?

• Is the candidate able to make judgments on matters of policy with the detachment of an outsider, one who has no career stake in the institution? If this person has children in the school, can he or she make judgments based on the good of *all* the children in the school?

• Can the candidate attend board meetings regularly and work on at least one committee of the board?

• Is the candidate interested enough in the work and purposes of the school to give generously of his or her talents and resources, whatever they may be?

• Is the candidate willing and able to become well acquainted with the school and its operations, and possibly privy to confidential information, yet able to keep from intervening in the daily affairs of the school?

• Is the candidate discreet and able to keep confidences?

Term of service

There are advantages to bringing new members regularly onto boards of trustees and to retiring those whose capacity to serve, or whose interest in serving, has declined to the point where others might serve better. Accordingly, most schools provide for fixed terms for trustees on a rotating basis. Many older schools that once had self-perpetuating boards of life members have changed their bylaws to the same effect. Usually the term of office is three to five years; sometimes a member goes off the board automatically after two or three terms for a period of one year before being eligible for re-election.

Some heads and trustees feel, however, that rotation has its price: losing wise leadership whose talents are committed to the school. During that one year off, able and useful people find that other demands on their talents take their time, and they may not be available for re-election when eligible. For these reasons, many boards exempt certain key officers — such as the chairman, treasurer, and recording secretary — from rotation.

Should the head or other educators be trustees?

Heads of schools may be full and regular members of their school's board, or members by virtue of their title — ex officio (with or without a vote) — or not members at all. We prefer the ex officio situation, as a simple matter of status and, more important, because the obligations and responsibilities of a regular trustee should not be assigned to the head, who is the professional leader of the school, and because the head ceases to be a trustee when ceasing to hold the job.

Whether a trustee or not, the head should attend all meetings of the board. If for some reason the board wishes to meet in executive session, without the head, the chairman should inform the head of the meeting and its purpose and, immediately after the meeting, of its results. It goes without saying that the head should receive copies of the minutes of all meetings. Executive sessions should be rare; if they are not, the school is in trouble.

Most people agree that an outside educator or two should be on the board — the head of another school, a college professor or dean, even a college president. It is helpful for the head and the trustees to have academic experience and an academic point of view represented on the board. If the educator is another school head, he or she should not be the head of a directly competing school or a close friend of the school's own head.

Representation of other groups

Now we come to the question of having on the board representatives of certain groups that have a direct and legitimate interest in the school and its policies and progress: graduates, parents, faculty, and students.

While we favor such representation for most schools, we also agree with those who see a fundamental difference between "representative" and "trustee." Whereas many graduates and parents may have all the qualifications listed above, teachers and students are less likely to. Surely they cannot meet the third qualification, that of making judgments on matters of policy with the detachment of an outsider, one who has no career stake in the institution. However, the advantages of the detachment of an outsider are complemented by the intimate, detailed knowledge of the school that students and teachers have and that the board often needs. The head also has this knowledge, of course, but in a somewhat different degree and way.

In orienting any faculty and student representatives on the board, it is wise to emphasize the importance of taking a global view of the school and its welfare and of avoiding the temptation to seem to speak for all the faculty or all the students. In most schools, a statement that starts with "The faculty thinks" or "The students think" is probably nonsense, for faculty and students are a varied lot and seldom think as one. Only when faculty and students have carefully discussed a policy and made a corporate decision on it can anyone say with truth what they think. When such corporate decisions are made, they should probably be reported by the head, not by a teacher or a student.

Thus faculty and student representatives to the board, like all other members, do best to speak only from their own information, experience, and judgment. They should not feel that they are on the board to give special representation to the interests of the group from which they are chosen, but rather that they accept, like any other trustee, general responsibility for the welfare of the board.

A further note about faculty and student representatives: It has not always been customary, especially in large, well-established schools, to have a faculty member on the board. Boards in general have had few contacts, formal or informal, with the teaching staff. For some years now, however, many faculties have wanted a share in the decision-making process or at least a chance to express their views. In a concurrent development, boards have become more aware than they used to be that good communication and understanding between faculty and trustees are of great importance and that they need the benefit of faculty opinion in many of their decisions. The number of schools that have provided for faculty membership on the board is approximately a quarter of the NAIS membership, and over half of these faculty representatives have the right to vote. Similar considerations have led to the provision by some schools for some form of student representation on the board. Others arrange for one or more students to attend meetings or parts of meetings as observers or, in effect, consultants.

Graduates are commonly represented on boards of independent schools. They may be elected to the board, usually for a fixed term, by either the graduates' association or the graduates in individual balloting, or they may be selected by the nominating committee of the board from a slate named by the association. Graduate representation on the board should include nomination and election procedures that will, so far as possible, ensure the selection of valuable trustees. Thus it is very desirable for the nominating committee to screen graduates who are candidates, since it is the nominating committee that has especially in mind the sorts of people and talents most needed by the board.

It is for the board itself to decide whether any or all of these groups shall be represented on the board and, if so, how the representatives shall be elected and for how long. Board membership is but one means of fostering two-way communication. From one point of view, it is too formal and narrow; more points of contact can be established through representation on board committees.

The important thing is to ensure communication with each group so that board members may be fully aware of attitudes and influences that have a strong bearing on the health of the school and their decisions concerning it. Alert school heads will see it as one of their responsibilities to keep ways open and provide opportunities for such communication and to be aware of communication gaps. The chairman of the board can also be very helpful in this area. The head and the chairman together probably are in closer touch than any others with all the elements of the school community.

2.

Board Committees

Much if not most of the work of the board is done by its standing committees. To them are brought almost all policy issues that will eventually be decided by the board. Before discussing these standing committees, however, we should look at one of the board's most important committees, one that does not, in the main, consider policy but rather considers who should be on the board and do the considering.

Nominating committee (committee on trustees)

In some schools, the nominating committee of the board is seen as a minor committee, perhaps composed of trustees for whom no other particularly useful service can be found. This is a grave mistake. The nominating committee, if it functions properly, has great importance, since it is responsible for the composition of the board and its committees. Over the years its decisions can spell the difference between a vital board and a weak one.

The nominating committee should be a standing committee of the board and have considerable continuity of membership from year to year. The school head and board chairman should be members ex officio because of their wide acquaintance with the community and their global view of the school's needs.

Because the functions and responsibilities of the nominating committee as described here are of far greater scope than most people envision, we suggest a broader title for this group: the committee on trustees. The committee ideally performs several functions, though it is realistic to say that in most schools the ideal is not reached. Here they are.

• The nominating committee maintains a list of possible board members and is constantly on the lookout for able people who might strengthen the board.

• The nominating committee considers the state of the board's membership and is aware of what sorts of people it needs in order to serve the school in the most competent way.

• As vacancies occur, either because of rotation policy or resignations, the nominating committee considers who of those available (or who can be persuaded to become available) can best fill them. The committee looks down the road a few years to try to match up likely vacancies with likely prospects.

• Before nominating a person to fill a vacancy, the chairman of the committee, one of its members, or the chairman of the board, perhaps even with the head of the school, talks with the prospective trustee so that they may exchange expectations of each other. Such preliminary talks should always be cleared with the board chairman. Board prospects should know in advance of nomination what duties and responsibilities they are likely to have and what special qualities and skills, if any, they are expected to bring to the board. Prospects, in turn, should speak of their expectations and how they see themselves able or not able to serve the board and the school. By establishing in advance of nomination whether the fit is likely to be a good one, frustration and disappointment can be avoided. It should be remembered that some competent and versatile trustees prefer to serve the school in areas different from those of their daily work; other trustees do not have any special field of competence but are able generalists, ready to give service and judgment where the need is greatest—vocational volunteers in the best sense.

• The nominating committee presents its slate to the board for election.

• The nominating committee takes responsibility for coordinating the orientation of new trustees (covered in the next chapter). In some schools, the board chairman and the head of the school do this job, but it can be up to the nominating committee to see that it gets done.

• After consulting the board chairman, board committee

chairmen, and each new trustee, the nominating committee assigns each new person to at least one standing committee of the board.

• The nominating committee evaluates the records of all trustees who are up for re-election and does not hesitate to suggest to those who have not served well, for whatever reasons, that they resign to make way for more active and useful members. In fact, at the end of trustees' terms and before any decisions are made about renewal, it is well to thank them for serving, ask them whether they wish to continue, and explore with them whether they feel they have been well used and able to make their best contributions to the school. The committee may also take charge of periodic evaluations of the performance of the board. (Trustee and board evaluation are covered in Chapter 4.)

Other standing committees

As we said earlier, to the standing committees should be brought almost all important items that will eventually be decided by the board. These committees hold the first group discussions of plans, issues, and problems. They identify and clarify the dimensions of the questions and elements needed for making sound decisions. In most cases, when these questions come before the full board, they should come with a committee recommendation, which may or may not be accepted by the board but which is the basis for beginning its discussion.

Many boards, especially in larger schools, say that no large decision may be made by the full board until it has first been considered by one of the board's committees. This rule prevents hasty action on questions that may have long-term effects on the school. Rule or no rule, board committees have, and should have, great influence, even though the power of final decision on major matters and establishing policy is, and must be, held by the full board.

Some boards have too many committees, too many meetings, and too much going over and over the same subject before a decision is made. Other boards have too few and thus lose the advantages of specialization and deep advance consideration of complex problems that accrue from the committee system. In schools having an organized committee structure, the committees listed below are usually found, sometimes under different names, and their functions are usually somewhat as described. Whether large or small or old or new, and whether the board has many committees, few, or none, the functions described below have to be provided for somehow. A wise board chairman, working with the nominating committee and the head, will see to it that there is appropriate delegation of responsibilities to members of the board and some specialization by them.

One other point: Committee membership should not be limited to members of the board, and for good reasons. By providing places on the appropriate committees for teachers or administrators, and for students, parents and graduates, and especially skilled and useful members of the community, a board can expand its contacts with these groups, get valuable help and involvement in the work and purposes of the school, and sometimes identify likely trustees. A committee chairman who is alive to such possibilities can increase contacts still further by inviting to meetings on an ad hoc basis others who can provide special knowledge of the subject being discussed.

If the committee system is to function properly, committees must meet when a problem needs study and, usually, when the next meeting of the full board needs a committee recommendation. Experience shows that someone—usually the board chairman or the head, and more often the head—must work closely with committee chairmen to keep things moving and perhaps at times to provide staff assistance. It is good policy to consider the chairman of the board and the head of the school ex officio members of all board committees, even though they should not be expected to attend all meetings.

Executive committee. This committee usually consists of four or five people, not necessarily the officers of the board. One of the main functions of the executive committee is to meet, either regularly or on call, to discuss problems and decisions that probably will be brought to the full board at some time in the future. The advantages of this kind of discussion are that it helps to clarify issues, shows where fuller information and documentation may be necessary, and helps the head of the school to decide whether or not, and in what form, various matters should come to the board.

It is very important, however, that the executive committee make actual decisions only in emergencies and that it never become a superboard or a policy-making group in itself. The danger of such a development is one reason many boards have no executive committee. There is no surer way to kill board members' interest than to have the executive committee do most of the planning and thinking; it soon divides the board into first- and second-class citizens.

The executive committee sometimes also functions as an informal long-range planning committee, proposing goals for the school. Further, it may consider before the finance committee does such broadly important things as the school budget, especially the salary scale, fringe benefits, tuition levels, and other financial areas that require a more inclusive point of view than might be taken by a typical finance committee. In schools where there is no executive committee, these kinds of financial matters are taken up by the advisory or personnel committee (see below) before going to the finance committee.

The executive committee may also be authorized to expedite the transaction of business between meetings of the board, especially when its members include the chairmen of other committees. All actions of the executive committee should be reported to the next meeting of the full board for discussion and approval—which prevents the executive committee from acting arbitrarily or in opposition to the wishes of the board as a whole.

Finance committee. This committee is concerned primarily with the financial management aspects of budget making. It usually bases its work on recommendations developed by the executive committee (or by the advisory or the personnel committee). The finance committee should work with the head and business manager in developing the budget. It should hear proposals for salary increases, which, in a well-established school, are most often reported to the committee not later than January for the coming school year and are then ratified by the board in January or February. The committee should also study the technical aspects of fringe benefits for the faculty and consider recommendations for changes in tuition and other student fees. In examining faculty and staff salaries and benefits, the committee should not forget to study those of the head.

(NAIS publishes annual statistics on salaries in independent schools; see Appendix A.)

Another responsibility of the finance committee is to arrange for and oversee the management and use of the school's operating and capital (endowment) funds. The day has passed when schools can afford simply to keep current cash in the bank; it must be invested and always working for the school. The day has passed, too, when an amateur group of trustees can be given responsibility for managing the school's investments. The finance committee must see to it that expert advice, perhaps from the trust department of a bank or other investment counsel, is sought and followed. The finance committee works in these areas closely with the head, the business manager of the school, and the treasurer of the board.

One of the most important policies to be established and periodically reviewed by the committee is how the proceeds from endowment, if any — interest and capital gains — are to be used and how returns can be tied in with orderly budget procedures. More and more schools today are adopting the policy of expecting a fixed return (say 5 per cent of the market value of the endowment averaged over a two-year period), no matter whether the actual return is more or less than that. This policy gives more stability to the process of budget making.

The finance committee, or often a *subcommittee on financial aid*, should make recommendations to the board concerning the school's financial aid program, the amount of money to be available each year for such aid, and its policy for making grants to individual students or families. (The School Scholarship Service, operated by the Educational Testing Service under a contract with NAIS, provides a means for determining financial need through a standard method of computation. Over 800 schools subscribe to this service and make grants in accordance with its principles.)

Recently, a number of schools have developed methods for making loans to students or their families, which are repayable after the students graduate from college. For schools, loans have an obvious advantage over grants; they are repaid. Thus schools are able to recycle their almost always inadequate supply of aid funds. The subject, an important one, is too complicated to be dealt with in detail here. The NAIS *School Loan Program Guide* gives information on developing loan policies and programs.

Decisions about financial aid often involve judgments about questions that can have significant effects on the whole school. What portion of the school's resources shall go into financial aid? To what categories of students shall the aid go? What qualifications shall the recipients of aid have? Since these questions go well beyond purely financial judgments and have to do with the nature and philosophy of the school, they should be considered also by some committee in addition to the committee on financial aid. Probably the executive committee should be consulted, possibly the long-range planning committee — if there is one — as well as the head and members of the staff, before a recommendation is made to trustees concerning financial aid. Also, it is good practice to have on the financial aid committee a few people in addition to staff members who can bring criteria other than financial ones into the discussion of making grants. The committee should not be directly involved in awarding grants to individual students; that should be done by the director of admission, director of financial aid, or others to whom the job is delegated.

The finance committee is also responsible for the school's insurance program, which must provide for a wide variety of contingencies and liabilities, including the possibility that trustees may be held liable for actions of the school. In view of the number of lawsuits being brought against schools, some form of "directors' and officers' liability insurance" is strongly recommended.

Buildings and grounds committee. This committee, whose duties are indicated by its title, should also work with and through the head and business manager as well as the superintendent of buildings and grounds, if the school has one. Many schools with extensive property have two separate committees, one for buildings and one for grounds. These committees, usually small, are composed of people who are interested and competent in these fields. When the school undertakes construction of a new building, the buildings and grounds committee usually works with the architect and contractor, although sometimes an ad hoc committee is formed for the purpose. Experience has shown, however, that one person, and one person only, should represent the school in dealings with architect and contractor; otherwise, confusion is inevitable.

Education committee. Most schools have an education committee whose purpose is to examine every aspect of the school's program in the light of the school's philosophy. This committee should include faculty representatives, and it might well have an outside educator or two, particularly if no educators are on the board. If the faculty has a curriculum committee, the education committee should work closely with it. The special role of the education committee should be to explore with head and faculty their ideas for improving the education provided by the school, encompassing every aspect of the school's program.

From time to time, the education committee may meet with a department of the school to learn more about the school's educational activities and courses. In so doing, it will be in a better position to inform the rest of the board of what the school is doing and to evaluate the head's and faculty's recommendations for change.

It is very important, however, that the committee not allow itself to get into the position of making judgments about specific curricular issues (shall we start Latin in seventh grade? shall certain elective mini-courses be given in grades 10-12? should formal grammar be introduced in the primary grades? or, even, should football be dropped?). These are properly decided by the faculty, which is professionally qualified for the task.

The proper balance between appropriate consideration and review and getting too deeply involved in what should be the professional duties of head and faculty is not easy to maintain. Not so long ago, educational policy in most schools was left largely to the head and faculty. Now, in many schools, this policy is becoming a central concern of trustees, and education committees are assuming corresponding importance. The educational world is full of diversity and experiment. Programs and methods that once went unquestioned are now strongly challenged. Both head and staff need the ideas and judgment of an intelligent group of lay people to hear and assess recommendations, to guide decisions, and to evaluate results. In addition, the education committee can help the board meet its responsibility of interpreting the school's program and policies to its constituencies.

A word of caution is needed here. The education committee sometimes becomes *the* committee because of its central role in educational policy making. Like the executive committee, it runs the danger of dividing the board into first- and second-class citizens. A strategy for avoiding this is to have one ad hoc committee study a particular question and another one, with somewhat different trustees, to study another particular problem, rather than having a standing education committee.

Development committee. This committee should supervise all fund-raising activities. Some boards delegate to the development committee the long-range planning for the school's development, including enrollment projections, plant expansion, endowment, and other aspects of growth and development. Since development planning leads to fund raising, however, other boards have delegated the planning function to the executive committee or to a long-range planning committee (see below) and only fund raising to the development committee. Either way, *all* fund-raising plans, by whatever group — graduates, parents, students — should be cleared by the development committee. If the school has a development director, this person works closely with this committee as its executive secretary.

Trustees, especially those on the development committee, should remember that development is much more than direct fund raising. It is concerned with what is generally referred to as "advancement" — all the ways in which the school presents itself to its constituencies and with the image of the institution, whether in its publications and mailings, reception of visitors, or the manner in which fund raising is carried out. The committee should not involve itself in operational details unless in some special circumstances it is specifically invited by a staff member to do so.

Later on we talk of the head's responsibility in fund raising. Here we must speak of the trustees' part, which is fully as important as the head's. All trustees of independent schools must be aware of the serious financial problems that face these schools and of the need for strengthening the financial sinews of their own school. So it can be said that, while in most aspects of the school's life program initiative and leadership must come from the head, in this special area the trustees cannot wait to be led but must take responsibility for helping to develop an overall plan and ensuring that all efforts are coordinated with those of the administration. They must match the head in determination to add new financial strength and, while giving the benefit of their judgment, must also give the encouragement of their understanding and support.

Once goals are defined and an effort to raise funds is approved, the board must work 100 per cent for its success. When a campaign is announced to the school's public, it should be possible to say that every trustee has made a pledge. Trustees must set an example of the kind of giving they expect from others and carry the main responsibility for campaigning, soliciting, and other parts of the program.

Other committees

The committee structure of many schools differs from what has just been described. Some schools make good use of the following sorts of committees, which, called by various names, may take on some or all of the functions of the more or less commonly known committees.

Advisory committee (head's committee). The main job of this committee is to hear, often in early stages, and in a most informal way, concerns and problems brought to it by the head. In some schools, this committee might also be involved in preliminary consideration of the budget. It is a committee to give advice, support, and reaction as the head feels the need of them. It is not always an action group, but it often does make recommendations to the board. Sometimes, though, its principal function is simply to help the head deal wisely with troublesome staff matters. In addition, the board may from time to time refer to the advisory committee questions that need discussion but do not fit the functions of any other committee.

The job of school head tends, in many respects, to be a lonely one, despite the fact that heads are usually surrounded by people. Heads need a few people with whom they can confer privately and in a relaxed way, knowing that what they say and discussion of it will be held in strict confidence. In some schools, the executive committee assumes the function of an advisory committee.

Personnel committee. Some schools make good use of a small committee that is responsible for discussing and sometimes making recommendations on the welfare and evaluation of the performance of the staff of the school. Items that may come under its aegis are those that might elsewhere come before the executive or advisory committee: salary levels, fringe benefits, housing, in-service training and staff development, policy on leaves, retirement, salaries, assistants, substitutes, and so forth. The committee may also help evaluate candidates for staff positions, determine how best to deal with staff people who should improve or leave, and provide a group for hearing faculty concerns when the head feels the need of such assistance.

Long-range planning committee. In a sense, the entire board should form the long-range planning committee, but many boards find it useful to have a special committee work with the head on planning for the future. This work involves projections for enrollment, annual and capital giving, buildings, grounds, and other areas. In the past, much long-term planning focused on plant expansion or improving facilities. Now, some schools are having to consider how to adjust to new circumstances by becoming smaller and reducing expenses, staff, and plant. Such planning for adjustment to smaller size and scope, however distasteful it may be to trustees, is much better than meandering aimlessly into extinction.

Another very important aspect of long-range planning concerns the review of the school's goals and policies established in the light of those goals. A model for long-range policy review was first developed in 1978 by the Commission on Educational Issues of NAIS. An overview describing the process, *Long-Range Planning for Independent Schools,* is available from NAIS. Also, NAIS and its member assocations can arrange for long-range planning policy workshops for schools seeking help in this very important area.

The hazards of committee meetings

A professional hazard, especially for school heads and board chairmen, is burnout, death by boredom, and ruination of family and recreational life by attending too many meetings. So, important as meetings are, their perpetrators should always ask, "Is this meeting necessary?"

We must not allow our committees to become groups that keep minutes and waste hours. Meetings should begin on time and stop promptly when business is finished so that hard-pressed members can get to their jobs, to their homes, or to bed. Desirable as the attendance of the head or board chairman may be, ways must be found to ease their burdens without making them feel guilty or disapproved of because they are absent. One way is to ask some other administrator to attend for the head and to have the vice chairman of the board share the chairman's duties, on a planned basis, with careful follow-up reporting to the head or chairman.

3.

Board Functions
and Duties

Before turning to the principal function of the board — policy making — we need to discuss two items of considerable importance to that function: the orientation of new trustees, to which too many schools give too little attention, and the special role of the board chairman.

Orientation of new trustees

In many schools, rotation of trustees results each year in boards getting several new members, usually inexperienced. Are these new trustees to sit silently, catching on during most of their first year and thus wasting part of their term? After all, if terms are short, new trustees might spend half of their first term getting acquainted and perhaps even making mistakes that could be avoided.

Rather than having a group of new members who can contribute little, a concerted effort must be made to help them be useful right away. The nominating committee, the chairman of the board, and the head of the school can all play a part, but the role of each should be made clear. One should be the principal planner and coordinator. Their goal is to produce effective trustees quickly.

Some schools have only one orientation session for their new trustees, while others have as many as three. In the case of three, they might be divided as follows.

Session 1. A general session during which each new trustee receives a full set of materials: the catalogue, booklet, or publicity piece or pieces about the school—what the school says about itself to the public; a history of the school; a statement of the school's philosophy; this trustee handbook; the bylaws of the school; the board's policy manual or a statement of how' the board functions; a list and statement of the functions of board committees; copies of recent board minutes to provide background on current issues; the school's policy book; the budget for the current year and, if available, a comparison with past budgets and a projection of future budget plans; a long-range planning report, if one exists; whatever brochures and public letters are available on annual and capital fund-raising plans, appeals, and results; a statement of the course of study or curriculum for all divisions of the school; a directory of parents and students; a list of parent and faculty committees; an organization chart showing how the various parts of the school interrelate and how the school is administered; a list of names, addresses, and home and office telephone numbers of all trustees; and a detailed map of the campus and of the interiors of buildings.

These materials should be reviewed and the trustees asked to read them—a job probably requiring several hours—before the next session or the next board meeting. The remainder of this first session can be spent in free discussion with the chairman and head of how the school works, the functions and responsibilities of the board, and guidelines for trustees as they may be called upon to work with faculty members, administrators, parents, and students.

Session 2. A session dealing primarily with the development program and the financial management of the school, with full, frank explanations and ample opportunity for sharing questions and concerns.

Session 3. A session on daily operations, including the curriculum, faculty organization and policies, student government and activities, rules and regulations, discipline, marks and reports, and so forth, followed by a tour of the premises, from most glorious auditorium or multipurpose facility through a sampling of classrooms, to the darkest corners of the boiler room, faculty lounge, or student recreation room. There should be no special sprucing up of the school for this tour. The object is to see the school as it really is.

The Park School
BROOKLANDVILLE, MARYLAND 21022

STATEMENT OF PHILOSOPHY AND OBJECTIVES

The Park School embodies in both its tradition and in its daily practice two assumptions: that human beings are capable of rational self-discipline, generosity, kindness, moral conviction, and concern for others; and that learning is an expression of positive energies and fulfills natural curiosity and impulse. Young people respond positively to the influence of these ideals, learning to trust and assert their own intellectual and moral powers, acquiring as they do a sense of confidence in themselves which will support a productive adulthood. Thus, the quality of expectation is most important, and the belief that positive expectations produce positive virtues is a fundamental point of doctrine.

This philosophy suggests or requires no single educational technique or methodology and may be manifested in the school in different ways. Whatever the method, however, the work of the school is sustained by the faith that the child contains inner strength, talents, and powers, which can be liberated and nurtured, and that the teacher's authority as an adult and as a scholar should be used not to suppress or constrain, but to provide the skills, the opportunities, the challenges, and the encouragement to bring about the flowering and fulfillment of the self in responsible freedom.

Thus considered, school activities become both ends in themselves and means toward more complex, more difficult ends. But however challenging and rigorous, school work need not be alienating or painful, nor need success be earned at the expense of others. Rather, academic achievement is the result of the use by the child, under proper stimulation and challenge, of the natural power of intellect, the exercise and application of which in itself provides pleasure and happiness.

Accepting these beliefs requires realistic and toughminded recognition of the problems they may bring—occasional disorder and untidiness, and of the intellectual errors to which they are liable—sentimentality, self-indulgence, egotism, and innocence.

To participate in the life of The Park School, as a parent, as a student, or as a teacher, requires trust in these good prospects, effort to maintain these positive expectations, and confidence that, under their influence, children will grow to adulthood, possessing the power to enact in their lives these beliefs about themselves and others.

These values and ideals underlie the following specific objectives and practices in the operation of the school:

I. AUTHORITY AND DISCIPLINE

In both academic and nonacademic matters it is the objective of the school to have learning occur as a mutual effort between students and teachers, such that students' energies and initiatives and strengths are encouraged and promoted, not limited and stifled.

It is the objective of the school to approach discipline and student behavior in such a way as to create conditions of moral and social growth in which a student acquires internalized discipline, autonomy, and self-control, based on reason, on a cooperative sense of community, and on a sympathetic understanding of the rights and needs of others.

II. INDIVIDUALISM

It is the objective of the school to offer a flexible curriculum and a rich, varied program of studies, and activities, and to support a high degree of involvement by teachers in advising and counseling students.

It is the objective of the school to foster individuality, to encourage respect for, and delight in, the uniqueness of each individual, and to be a place where plain speaking, honesty, and authenticity govern all relationships.

III. SCHOOL AND SOCIETY

It is the objective of the school to teach those skills and encourage those traits of character which enable successful achievement in a society undergoing constant social and technological change, changes which demand both accommodation and critical scrutiny.

It is the objective of the school that, in their attitudes toward their work, students should strike a balance between competition for success in the world's eyes, and learning for personal and intrinsic satisfaction.

It is the objective of the school that students should acquire the conviction that learning is an active and fulfilling process, to be pursued throughout life.

It is the objective of the school to prepare students in the broadest sense, not only for further academic achievement, but also for the continuing process of choosing for themselves from the widest range of possibilities life offers.

IV. COMMUNITY

It is the objective of the school that these values, reflecting as they do the adaptation of the aspirations and goals of the original founders and benefactors of the school to conditions of contemporary life, should remain the center of its educational program, thereby allowing the school to serve a community of those who understand and endorse this philosophy as a basis for the education of their children.

December 11, 1989

TO: Nominating Committee

FROM: Nancy Rhoads, Head

There will be a meeting of the Nominating Committee of the School Committee on Thursday, January 4, 1990, at 7:45 p.m. at John Wilkinson's home, 470 E. Locust Ave.

Agenda: 1. Review current panels

2. John Stine and Leanna Whitman will be rotating off

3. Place Andy Sharpless and Pat Macpherson on subcommittees

4. Set April meeting to review subcommittees to be completed by May 1.

RSVP: Nancy Rhoads
248-1263 *replied — may be late*
12-20-89

member of Gtn Mtg
_____

Phil Ford

member of another
mtg
_____

Russ Endo
Ron   "
Tom Unckeford
Joe Evans
Dian Fatula

non-friend
_____
* Allen Wilson
   Melvin Bream (?)
   Andy Williams
   Ed Zubrow

The board chairman

How well a board of trustees functions depends considerably on the chairman. Ideally, if the chairman has a deep interest in the school and time to spend on its affairs and is wise, clear, and understanding, then the board and its committees are likely to function well and the school's policies to be soundly developed, well understood, and consistently followed. The board's relations with the head of the school are characterized by openness, mutual understanding, and respect. The school's long-range planning is under control, its annual and capital fund raising are well led (though not generally by the chairman), and its relations with its clientele and the community are in good order. Additions to the board are wisely selected, the talents of members are well used, and the trustees understand the principles by which they as individuals should be guided in their relations with the school head, faculty members, parents, community, and the board itself.

In a well-run school, head and chairman work closely together, communicate frequently and freely, and each understands the other and carries an appropriate part of the burden of leadership in a spirit of reciprocal confidence and respect. However, the chairman must never become, or seem to others to be, so closely identified with the head of the school that he or she loses, or seems to lose, independence of judgment. Such a loss, whether apparent or real, is a loss to the school and may jeopardize the confidence people have in its governance. There is no place for blind faith; clear-seeing mutual respect is what is needed.

Board chairmen do not, and should not, serve forever. In fact, some schools have found that terms of three to six years work best. Much depends upon how seasoned the head is. Also, sometimes the best candidates for chairman are willing to serve only for a limited period. However, terms shorter than three years often do not work well because of the seasoning needed for a chairman to reach full effectiveness. At any rate, the board, and especially its nominating committee, should be aware of the need to keep developing new board leadership and not wait for the crisis of resignation before looking for a competent successor.

Policy development: the board's most important function

While some of the time in board meetings may be devoted to hearing and discussing reports, and individual trustees may, alone or with others, perform specific pieces of work for the school, their essential task as a group is to make policy. The head of the school and staff should review points that might reach the board and its committees to make sure that these are related, directly or indirectly, to questions of policy and that they are not routine, repetitive items. For example, a board should set policy for appointing staff members, but the administration should make the actual appointments (except that of the head) in accordance with these policies, keeping the board advised of all changes. The board should approve appointment qualifications, salary levels, staff classification plans, and, possibly, number of employees by grade authorized in the budget, but it should not approve lists of individual appointments and promotions.

It is good practice to require that every major item of business and policy first be referred to an appropriate committee of the board for study and recommendation before it comes to the whole board, except in urgent circumstances where immediate decision is necessary, and these should be rare.

Basic ingredients. Trustees serve without compensation and spend much valuable time on school business. To make the best use of their time on behalf of the school, they need continuing staff assistance, not only to provide secretarial services, but also to review and document items for board consideration, to prepare the agenda, and to develop policy recommendations for board deliberation. Most preparation and staff work must be done by the head or delegated to those whom the head supervises.

In the paragraphs that follow, we have in mind a school that is well enough established and large enough for the head to have staff to help in the process of working with the board. In many small schools, however, the head has hardly any staff, perhaps only a school secretary, a receptionist, and a part-time bookkeeper. In such schools, much of the staff work that the board needs has to be done by others; schools should be grateful for trustees who are able to give assistance here, either by doing the work themselves or having paperwork done by secretaries in their own offices. However a school goes about carrying out the steps recommended below, these must be planned and coordinated by the head, with the chairman of the board being kept in touch and consulted when necessary.

Proposals by the head. Policy making and planning must be closely related. Policies considered and approved by the board must be compatible with plans for the school's future, which the board must also consider and approve. Accordingly, the key administrators and department heads who report to the head should take part in proposing policies, particularly for their own areas. These policies should not be just those required to solve immediate problems but should constitute a total policy framework.

More and more schools have long-range planning committees that meet regularly to discuss and recommend immediate and long-range goals and then to review and revise these goals once a year. On such committees, boards may have representatives of all interested groups — trustees, administrators, faculty, graduates, parents, and students.

Only when the head and staff propose policies for board consideration, as well as long-range plans for the principal activities of the school, can a board apply most effectively its varied experience and analytical talents to considering the factors affecting the school's future. With this type of staff assistance, a board can spend its time and energy on matters of primary importance to the school and not get bogged down in consideration of details.

It is good policy for heads to have all trustees posted in advance on major items coming up for consideration even when a board committee has already acted favorably on a policy proposal. The more information trustees have before a meeting, the more likely they are to make the best use of their time and to act with good judgment on proposals made to them. Many boards avoid making hasty and ill-considered decisions by not taking action at a meeting on anything that was not on the agenda circulated in advance of the meeting, or at least considered by a board committee and brought to the full board with the committee's recommendation. If a policy issue is brought up without notice by a trustee in a full board meeting, it may be discussed right then in a preliminary way, but it should be referred to a committee for further consideration, with all the needed information, and then be brought to the board at a later meeting with well-developed recommendations.

Policy book. Trustees, as well as school heads and others connected with the school, are helped in their deliberations if a book or manual of school policies is kept and periodically brought up to date as new board and administrative decisions are made. Without a written record of approved policies, both staff and board may spend considerable and often futile effort in trying to see what action the board may already have taken on questions that arise. Unless board minutes are indexed, which they should be each year, it is difficult to pinpoint earlier policy decisions.

A policy book does not need to be formal or elaborate, although it may be. Either way, it must be kept up to date. One easy way is to file excerpts from the board's minutes, with decisions classified by subject. Several copies should be kept, with the original never leaving the head's office.

Typical subjects for inclusion in such a collection are bylaws, school objectives, board organization, admission and financial aid policy, finance and budgeting procedures, staffing and personnel policy, school organization and administration, and curriculum.

The relation of the board to the head also needs to be spelled out in the policy book. Many heads are not sure just which matters require board approval and consequently send more or fewer items to the board than may be necessary or desirable. Again, heads sometimes do not understand their responsibility and that of the staff for developing policies for the board to approve and use in their oversight of the head's work. Too often policies are developed piecemeal only as problems arise. Often there is lack of regular reporting back to the board on actions it has voted. The policy book can prescribe a reporting procedure and assign responsibility to administrative staff members for following up on board actions.

Informing the board. Certain items, like the budget or slate of nominees to fill board vacancies, must always come to the board for consideration and approval. It is helpful for trustees and for administrators to establish a calendar showing when important routine items must be discussed and decided so that plans can be made for the coming year. Such a calendar is especially helpful when major changes in staff or board officers, particularly the chairman, take place.

Regular reporting enables the board to evaluate the various phases of the school's activities. In carrying out its responsibility to supervise and guide the school's operation—responsibility that has been delegated to the head and staff—the board should do far more than just keep an eye on the periodic statements of income and expense and the balance sheet. Needing to evaluate the school in its many parts and as a whole, the board must depend in large part on reports prepared by the head and staff. These reports may be written or oral, formal or informal; their purpose and effect should be to keep the board well informed.

Evaluation reports. Periodically, and in some sort of rotation, the head should ask key staff members to prepare a confidential report for the head and the board that describes accomplishments, needs, and problems in their respective areas of responsibility. The head may then coordinate these reports in another report that gives his or her own views regarding overall accomplishments, problems, and plans for the future. This method, properly used, serves as a regular stock taking and frame of reference for the administration and for the board. The reports do not need to be prepared and submitted at any one time; they may be spread over an entire school year or even over two or three consecutive years.

Statistical reports. So that the board may evaluate reports furnished to it and be kept informed on various phases of the school's work, the head or someone the head designates—in a small school, it might even be a volunteer trustee—should regularly provide statistical data on the school's operations. These statistics should form a historical series, with interpretation where necessary. Once started, such charts can be readily updated. Statistical measures that might be used are

> Admission: number of applicants and for what grades; number admitted and to what grades; number of minority students; number of students of the other sex, in the case of a recent change to coeducation; number of stu-

dents receiving some form of financial aid; number of children of graduates, or younger brothers and sisters, applying and number and per cent of each accepted; geographic and neighborhood application trends; number of withdrawals and reasons

Teachers: experience and academic qualifications

Student-faculty ratio

Courses: titles, number of courses, class section sizes

Testing: scores on standardized tests of academic aptitude and achievement, grade by grade, including College Board tests or those of American College Testing (ACT)

College placement records or, for schools not going through grade 12, placement in other schools

Faculty salaries: levels, ranges, medians, benefits, perquisites

Cost per student of services: admission, athletic department, meals, etc.

Fund raising: annual giving, capital giving

Writing things down

Having school policies, reports, lists, and statistical information written down keeps things straight and clear, bolsters weak memories, helps keeps arguments based on fact rather than speculation, and provides for continuity in times of extensive changes in board and staff and for a kind of soundness in times when mismanagement needs to be dealt with. It can, however, be dangerous to have too many things written down, especially in elaborate detail, for the written document can become a substitute for thinking — thinking about important new problems as they come up, thinking about new solutions appropriate to new circumstances. Some school people take a certain comfort in being able to turn to the text to find the old answers.

Also, because ours is a litigious age, people may resort to what one head calls "a rush to the text" instead of making an effort to work out the best solution. A rush to the text can inhibit the sort of global thinking about the problems and opportunities of a school that helps people arrive at creative solutions that are best for everyone, not for a particular special interest. Further, having too many recorded letters of the law can be an unhealthy substitute for communication. A constantly fresh, honest exchange of ideas among all groups is essential to a healthy, creative school.

Government regulations

The board needs periodic reports on federal, state, and local regulations and legislation that involve nonpublic schools, including developments in aid programs provided by federal, state, and local governments. In addition to their other duties, heads must keep posted on this increasingly influential area of concern. The board, or certain board members, may well be asked to join with other schools in pressing for certain legislation or in opposing unwelcome legislation—a form of cooperative effort that appears to be increasingly necessary in many states and on the federal level. In some schools, one trustee is assigned as a one-person committee to keep up on legislative developments, to work with the head, and to report to the board, with recommendations for action if needed.

The board should also arrange to keep in touch with metropolitan, state, and regional associations of independent schools, many of which have a staff member or volunteers who keep informed about what is going on in the halls and offices of government and who bring to the attention of government people—both legislators and civil servants—the needs and concerns of the schools. Quite often this keeping in touch is done by school heads as they meet and talk, but assistance from a qualified trustee or two can be invaluable.

More about the board's evaluation of the school

We have already made clear that an important duty of the board is to evaluate the school and have suggested some ways to do it. It must be clear to any intelligent observer that assessing the quality of a school is a difficult task because much of the evidence contained in the reports and communications recommended here is certain to produce differences of opinion and interpretation. Furthermore, the quality of the product can hardly be measured the way automobiles coming off an assembly line are inspected for mechanical efficiency, safety, and durability. A school is not static, so it cannot be examined from various angles in a testing laboratory, although tests can and should be applied to it; it is moving and dynamic, generating dozens of different reactions and attitudes, and for a multitude of reasons.

The board must, nevertheless, do its best to judge the school's performance. Here are some suggestions on how to approach the task.

• Evaluation has to be a continuing process, not an effort to render a judgment on the school as a whole or in a given moment in time.

• Assessment should follow the outline of the school's declared philosophy and purpose.

• The board should have an opportunity to learn, from time to time, what is happening in similar schools across the country, what trends are revealed, and what significant new programs or policies are on the horizon. NAIS provides annual statistical data to each school through its head and board chairman. In addition, the NAIS Trustee Committee conducts regional seminars for trustees and heads, provides a day of programs for trustees at the NAIS annual conference, responds to requests for information, and develops special projects to improve trusteeship.

• One of the most significant measures of a school's performance is to be found in the opinions of its graduates. Many schools make it a practice to poll recent graduates periodically, asking them to assess their experience in school, the strengths and weaknesses of the program as it was in their time, and what they estimate to have been the school's overall influence on them.

• Through teachers, students, and parents, the board should try to get the "feel" of the school—a sense of faculty and student morale, of the skill and dedication of the teachers, of the students' spirit, of their interests in the school and what goes on in it. Assessment in this all-important area is likely to come out of the collective and cumulative opinions of all the board, gained through their various contacts over a period of time rather than stemming from a calculated effort in any given year. School visits, discussed below, play a part here.

• Unprejudiced observers can be very helpful. Many schools are visited periodically by committees of their regional accrediting association or their own independent school association. The reports of these visits deserve careful study. The board should realize, however, that evaluation by colleagues from other schools can be exercises in mutual backscratching. A strong school, or a school that earnestly wants to improve, makes sure that the visiting committee sees the institution as it normally is, not temporarily polished, and attempts to identify in advance the problems and weaknesses on which it wishes to have the visiting committee's advice.

• The school may also engage one or more consultants to visit it and provide an outside evaluation of the school as a whole or of its performance in particular areas. It is essential that the consultants be competent in the field they are being asked to evaluate and that they be encouraged to be honest and frank. Otherwise, they are not worth the money they cost and the anxiety they arouse. Instructions to consultants should be as clear and precise as possible, and planning the project should, from the beginning, be done with the full understanding and cooperation of the head. The head should work out the details, including a statement of costs, before the consulting work begins.

Trustee responsibilities to school constituencies

Each trustee holds in trust the welfare of the school and should feel responsible in the largest sense for promoting the school. Trustees are responsible to the parents, the students, the faculty, the graduates, the patrons, and to the society from which the school derives its independence.

Responsibility to parents. In the few schools that are parent-owned or parent-controlled, some or all of the trustees are elected by the parents. In most schools, however, boards are self-perpetuating. They elect all or most of their members, some of whom may be parents of current or former students. In many schools, the head or chairman submits an annual written report to parents covering major activities and developments of the year, often including budget and projections.

Responsibility to students. Since a school exists to provide sound education for its students, trustees are responsible for the students' welfare. The board's responsibility to students is carried out chiefly through powers delegated to the head and the faculty. Because modern students' interest in their education tends to be clear and lively, the wise board will find formal and informal ways of consulting students and exchanging views frankly and honestly with them. One way is for a member or two of the education committee to sit in on occasional student council meetings to get student points of view and interpret board actions. Another way is very informally while visiting the school. In their contacts with students, trustees need to be very careful not to interfere or even seem to interfere in the operations of the school.

Responsibility to the faculty. The board is surely responsible for the welfare of the faculty. The school must attempt to the best of its ability to provide adequate salaries and fringe benefits, physical plant and equipment, and other facilities for the proper functioning of the educational program. This kind of responsibility is usually understood by trustees, but the relationship should not stop there. Most boards now recognize the importance of furthering the professional development of the faculty, including the head, by budgeting for summer courses or travel to enrich teaching, for attendance at professional meetings, for visits to other schools, and for sabbatical leaves. The temptation to loosen a tight budget by removing such allowances has to be resisted, for they help keep teachers enthusiastic, on their toes, and growing.

NAIS recommends that a designated amount of the school's total operating budget be allocated each year to activities that promote professional growth and development. NAIS and other professional organizations offer workshops and services for teachers during the school year and the summer that address the special interests of teachers of mathematics, social studies, writing, and reading, librarians, the special needs of students at various ages, teaching methods and classroom management, curriculum building, and various aspects of administration for heads and other school administrators. The NAIS annual conference, regional conferences of independent schools and professional associations, and university courses also offer opportunities for professional development, personal refreshment, and stimulation.

Responsibility to graduates. Since many graduates remain interested in their school and contribute to its welfare, they are entitled to regular reports. Most schools have a magazine giving news of the school and its graduates. In addition, at certain meetings of graduates and especially through a special annual report of the head that is mailed to all graduates, parents, and friends, the board's stewardship should be reported. If these groups are to be asked to support the school through annual giving and capital fund campaigns, they are entitled to a full report from the school's management that describes the financial condition of the school, gifts received during the past year, and the board's and administration's plans for the future. This kind of information, while it may be provided by the head, is in fact a report from the trustees.

Responsibility to friends. What has just been said applies fully to friends and patrons, both past and prospective. Here also should be included former trustees, for whom some schools arrange occasional special meetings for reporting and discussion. At any rate, it is the board's responsibility to see that these groups are fully informed.

Responsibility to society. Finally, the board is responsible to the community in which the school is located and to our democratic society, which makes possible the existence of independent schools. The tax-exempt status of independent schools, and their freedom to experiment with educational techniques and philosophy, require that trustees be conscious of their responsibility to share the results of promising experiments, to broaden enrollment through recruitment of students from nontraditional sources and through financial aid, and to work with the public schools in every way possible to improve education. Schools do not themselves build a better world, but they do build the builders.

A note about small schools

We have spoken about the responsibility of boards of trustees to find the resources to establish adequate salaries for head and staff and to see to it that the school is administered by a strong, well-organized staff. We recognize, however, that many quite small schools have no well-established clientele, no endowment, and no well-to-do patrons or trustees. They must operate on a shoestring and depend in large measure on a strong spirit of volunteerism among their community. Nevertheless, the boards of these schools have the same responsibility to their constituencies that the boards of more established schools do.

Visits, voices, and volunteers

Before we discuss relations between the board and the head of the school, five other specific items need to be dealt with to help trustees function properly.

Visits to the school. Visits to the school are a valuable source of information to trustees during their terms of service. This can be encouraged in a number of ways. One is to have an annual or periodic trustees' visiting day, when all who can do so are expected to visit. A disadvantage of this plan is that trustees inevitably see the school trying extra hard to do and look its best. They can, however, learn much from seeing what people consider to be their best. Another way is to pass around at each board meeting a schedule of visiting days — all days, not just certain days — asking trustees to sign up. This advance commitment helps defeat procrastination or competition with daily urgencies. Yet a third way is simply to keep reminding trustees that they are welcome to visit the school at any time and urging them to do so with or even without notice if they can plan or happen to be near the school. Although teachers usually prefer to know about visits in advance, their preference need not determine visiting policy.

It is important for trustees and school staff members to understand that the purpose of visits is to broaden trustees' knowledge of the school, not to evaluate. If teachers, students, and others feel that a trustee is there to inspect and criticize, discomfort and much less open, honest sharing of information are likely to result. The purpose of visits should be for trustees to see things as they are and to store away facts and impressions gained, which, along with all the other information they have, can be used to make judgments about school policy and how well it is being carried out.

Most schools do not object to having trustees ask to come to visit classes and talk with students and others to learn more about the school, what people do there, and how they feel about it.

It is helpful, too, for trustees to look at the school in the light of its current purposes and policies, not to compare it with the way it used to be when they were there, whenever that may have been. This is especially important in the lower grades, where "up front" teaching is much less likely than it used to be, with students tending to be much more on their own and the teacher acting more as plan coordinator. Vital questions to ask: What is the plan in the classroom? How are the people, space, materials, and time organized? How much learning seems to be going on?

If visiting trustees see something that they don't understand, disapprove of, or believe goes contrary to school policy, they should wait to discuss it, in due season, with the head. Heads should be grateful to know what trustees have seen and have a chance to explain or, if need be, to take appropriate action when and as they think best. Schools, being full of human beings, are never perfect.

Talking with people in the school community. Another valuable source of information for trustees is the people of all generations in the community who know or know of the school and have views to express or experiences to report. Trustees can listen, ask questions, absorb, and perhaps occasionally interpret. Trustees who are parents of students in the school will, of course, learn a great many things about what goes on, as interpreted by very involved young minds. The important thing is to listen, to hear, to understand, and to store away information and feelings so that they may become a part of the general wisdom of the board.

Dealing with complaints. In any school, some of the people are bound to be unhappy some of the time. In most cases, dissatisfaction is dealt with by direct discussion by the staff with the parents, students, or others involved. Inevitably, however, trustees will from time to time receive complaints from disgruntled parents, and even sometimes from a disgruntled teacher or student. Trustees should never attempt to solve the problem but, after listening, refer the person complaining directly to the head.

Trustees should listen, however, so that complainers know

they are being heard. If the trustees are sure they are on sound ground, they may explain school policies. But their only advice should be that complainers address their concerns to the teacher or other person involved, or to the head. The trustees' duty then is to inform the head — only the head — that someone has complained and what the complaint is. If the complaint comes in writing, any written answer should say that the question is being referred to the head and indicate that a copy of the reply is being sent to the head.

If the matter is particularly sticky or serious, or if the complainer has already spoken to the head and still feels dissatisfied, the trustee may then turn the matter over to the chairman of the board, and the chairman may take it up with the head to try to work out the best way to deal with the problem. The main point is that trustees must never circumvent the head, even with the best of intentions. The board chairman has a particular responsibility to keep trustees in line in this respect and to clarify and reclarify the proper division between responsibilities between board and staff.

Handling the negative story. Although disaster and crisis are fortunately rare in independent schools, they sometimes do occur. It is therefore wise to plan in advance how information about such events should be communicated to the media and the school's constituencies. The key to handling communications in a crisis is the ability to balance the right and responsibility of the media to report the news with the school's right and responsibility to keep on running as an educational institution. Here are some guidelines.

• Try to know important media representatives ahead of time. It is useful to invite editors and education writers to the school from time to time to learn about and discuss program, problems, and other aspects of school life.

• Have a written plan for crisis management within the school.

• If time permits when a negative story is imminent, assemble a small group to determine the facts and to determine whether the problem really is a crisis. Don't rush to respond to what someone else might interpret as a crisis.

• Designate one person, preferably the head or the board chairman, to speak for the school.

- Share what is a matter of public record immediately, recognizing that these facts will come out anyway and that it is preferable to have them released on the *school's* terms.
- Have all information attributable to a person or to a readily available document.
- Remember that information that could be legally damaging to an individual, especially if that person is a minor, should be kept confidential.
- Be sure to share immediately with trustees and key volunteers any information given out so that they may hear it in advance and not only on the six o'clock news.
- Keep a detailed journal of what happened and what was reported to the media and to the school's constituents.
- When dealing with radio and television, choose a representative who is cool and commanding under pressure. Subtle subconscious public reactions may be as important in the long run as the statements themselves.
- As soon as the crisis begins to resolve itself, send a letter of full explanation to the entire constituency—graduates, parents, and friends. They will want to lend their support, but they need information to do so.

Trustees who want to give extra time. Some trustees, especially those who do not work full time and enjoy volunteering their services, say they find pure policy making, unrelieved by concrete work done for the school, dull and insufficiently rewarding. Their interest and sense of usefulness, as well as their knowledge of the school, grow if they can help organize or help with specific tasks and services. They will soon find themselves part of a larger group of volunteers—parents, students, teachers, people in the community. When trustees serve as volunteers, especially inside the school, they must not forget that they are volunteers helping the school, not trustees making policy. They are, while volunteering, employees.

4.

The Board
and the Head

We have already emphasized that a clear understanding of the respective responsibilities of board and head is fundamental to the smooth functioning of a school's administration. This chapter concentrates on the board in its relations with the head. While policy formulation is clearly the responsibility of the trustees, they should not only give weight to the views of the head but, to a great extent, rely on the head for initiative and leadership as well.

Responsibilities of the head

School heads differ, and grow, and grow different; none is omniscient or omnicompetent; and a school and its board, if they are to make the most of their resources, must build around the strengths and weaknesses, the interests and lacks of interest, and the personality and idiosyncrasies of the head. There is no single right pattern of responsibilities. When a school changes heads, the pattern changes; as a head develops, the pattern goes on changing.

This understood, it can be said again that it is the duty of the head to carry out the policies established by the governing board and to serve as the professional educational leader of the institution. Certain areas of the head's responsibility can be clearly spelled out.

Planning the school's future. The head of the school, with the help of whatever committee is in charge of long-range planning, is responsible for developing plans for the near- and long-term future of the school. These plans include such important factors as enrollment objectives, course offerings, class size, faculty size, plant additions or necessary alterations, and financial requirements.

After the proper committees have developed and recommended plans, these should be reviewed and approved by the board. They should be projected for perhaps five years ahead and be reviewed and updated every year. Emergencies or sudden changes, especially in smaller, less established schools, may require planning for a crucial next six months.

Enrollment. The head is responsible for the enrollment and for handling admission, though in most schools this task is delegated to a director of admission. If the school is new and small, and if active promotion and recruitment of students are required, prime responsibility for planning rests with the head. Trustees should be willing to help and probably can be extremely helpful with some prospects, but the basic responsibility is the head's.

Admission. The head and the school's admission committee—which should be a staff committee, not a board committee—must have the sole and final responsibility of deciding which students to admit, acting in accordance with basic admission policies established by the board. Trustees often receive pressure from friends on behalf of applicants, particularly if admission is highly competitive. The head or admission director should be glad to hear from trustees who can add significant information concerning a family and a candidate, but, again, they must have the last word on admission of individual students.

Discipline. Although teachers have the principal responsibility for student discipline, and the heads of the various divisions of the school also play an important part, the head of the school must assume ultimate responsibility for the discipline of students. Discipline, especially in cases of suspension and dismissal, should be based on due process—procedural fairness—and on published policy guidelines. If discipline is poor, head and staff must resolve the problem, and the trustees have every right to hold them responsible.

Dismissal of students. The head must have the right to dismiss any student who, in the judgment of the head and school officials, should be separated from the school for academic reasons or for unsatisfactory behavior. As a matter of discretion, tact, and good communication, the head may on occasion notify trustees of an impending action or of an action taken, not to ask their permission, but to inform them so that they can answer any questions that may come to them.

Due process. The right of independent schools to dismiss or suspend students is sometimes challenged by parents, and a number of due process suits have been brought against schools by aggrieved students or parents. It is important for boards and heads of schools to develop policies that ensure for students their right to due process and protect them from arbitrary or capricious exercise of authority.

In the eyes of the law, an implied contract exists between a school and its students whereby the school obligates itself to provide a good education within the terms of its philosophy and established practices, descriptions of which should be published, and the students obligate themselves to abide by the rules and requirements of the school. These rules, a condition of admission, should be published, as should the specific grounds for suspension or expulsion.

Students and their parents have the right to a fair hearing, and schools have an obligation to show cause for suspension or expulsion. In schools where communication among parents, students, and staff is good, where disciplinary problems are recognized early, where attempts are made to deal with them constructively before they become critical, and where careful, written records of serious events are kept so that evidence is clear, trouble is unlikely to arise.

The ideal objective is to have all parties agree that the disciplinary action undertaken by the school is in the interest of the student's development in the broadest sense. School heads need to be aware of all these considerations. Alert school heads have an early warning system for situations that have the potential for major conflict. It is helpful to explain school policies clearly during admission interviews. In general, courts respect the actions of schools that handle serious discipline problems according to procedures deemed fair and reasonable under the law.

Financial aid. The head, or some member of the staff to whom this responsibility is delegated, should discuss financial aid with parents who request it and inform them of the policy of the board. To determine the extent of need, it is common practice to ask parents to complete a standard financial aid form for review by the designated members of the staff, who base their decision on board policies.

If a financial aid committee of the board exists, it should not review individual cases but should be sure that the school's policies are fair and that they are modified by the board when the need arises. Only cases that raise some issue of policy or a difficult area of judgment should be discussed by such a committee. This process provides an objective basis for awarding grants and removes grant making from the realm of personal negotiation.

Whatever a school's policy on financial aid for faculty children may be — and considerable variation in practice exists — grants to faculty children should be determined according to the same criteria that are used for other applicants for financial aid. Thus faculty parents should submit, using the Parents' Financial Statement or other standard form, the same information about their financial status that other parents do.

Growing numbers of schools are acknowledging the importance of financial aid by creating the position of director of financial aid, rather than having an admission officer, other staff member, or faculty member perform this function. Good use of the school's resources is more likely to be made by someone trained in financial aid procedures than by someone who can give only partial attention to this task.

Relations with faculty members. The head should be left free to employ teachers and other staff members without having to present alternative candidates for the board's consideration. The head must take responsibility for appointing the best people to be found at salaries within the established salary range, scale, or policy laid down by the board.

Individual salaries of new teachers have to be set by the head in accordance with a salary schedule, if the school has one. Salaries of the faculty, but not of individuals, may be reviewed by the finance or personnel committee so that trustees may see that the general policy of advancing teachers on the salary scale is being observed.

If the head wishes to create a new position of some importance to the school, such as director of studies or assistant head, he or she should discuss it with the appropriate trustee committee before discussions or interviews with candidates take place.

Dismissal of teachers. An increasingly difficult area of decision is dismissal of teachers because of incompetence, change of program, or need to reduce staff. The head is wise to have a clear policy on these matters and to get it considered, written down, and approved by the board. It is important to record evidence and to counsel the teacher involved as early as possible.

The head must not forget that teachers as well as students have the right to due process. It is well for the head to recommend to the board policies for respecting that right.

Publicity. The head should be responsible for and supervise all publicity for the school. This task must be delegated, since most heads, except in very small institutions, cannot possibly do it along with all their other responsibilities. A trustee who works in public relations, journalism, or advertising can often be extremely helpful and make a useful contribution by undertaking some or all of the work involved. Regardless of who does the work, however, the head should assume responsibility for the overall supervision of press releases and statements to the public.

Financial affairs. A school budget is always more than an estimate of income and expense for a given period of time, for it also reflects the educational philosophy of the school. Therefore, the head should always take the lead in preparing the budget, assisted by the business manager. The budget should be prepared from the bottom up with the assistance of the people responsible for the various cost centers, especially department and division heads. But the head of the school is the one to set limits and say no. This cannot be the function of the business manager, even though a business manager who is experienced can greatly assist the head in setting limits and helping to develop an understanding of the need for such limits. Together, the head and the business manager should present their proposals to the finance committee of the board, which should satisfy itself regarding their soundness.

Once the finance committee and the board of trustees have approved the annual budget, the business manager, the head, and others empowered to spend money should be free to do so within the limits of the budget without having to consult the trustees about expenditures. Good budget control depends on prompt preparation of monthly expense figures, with totals for the year to date and comparisons with the previous year's figures and with projected figures for the current year. The head, the chairman, and the board's finance or executive committee can properly expect the business manager to make such figures available monthly, or at least quarterly.

Maintenance of property. The head is responsible for seeing that routine maintenance and repair of the physical property are carried out. Since the head and staff are on the grounds daily, and the trustees are not, it is up to the head to see that the buildings and grounds committee is informed of any unusual conditions affecting the property of the school.

Health and safety. The head is responsible for the health and safety of students while they are under the school's jurisdiction. The school's own health and safety regulations must satisfy the requirements of state and local authorities.

Fund raising. To what extent is the head responsible for fund raising? Must the head raise the money for needed projects, or is this a trustee function? Can a head refuse to help raise money on the grounds that the job is an academic one and therefore the head cannot leave the school for outside activities? The truth lies at neither extreme. In all aspects of school administration, the head must exercise leadership, but he or she needs the active support of the trustees as well as of graduates and parents.

The head should be alert to the developing needs of the school and the money needed to strengthen the program and plant. The head must talk over these requirements with the proper committees of the board and with the board itself, and together they must decide on the ways and means to raise the funds. But if there is any part of the school's activity in which trustees should take strong and even operational leadership, it is that of fund raising. The head's time should be reserved for crucial contacts and solicitations. The head's place is *in* the school, helping to make it worthy of receiving gifts. The head can be of great value in undertaking the cultivation of a few major long-term prospects by writing special letters and perhaps making a yearly visit to those who live far away or cannot be directly involved in the life of the school.

In a large capital campaign, it may pay the school to employ reputable fund-raising counsel to advise about the perceptions and concerns of the constituency and the amount that might be raised and to supervise the mechanics of carrying out the campaign and making best use of workers. Special counsel may not be needed, however, where one or two people in the school community have had successful experience and can devote ample time to the campaign, where the number of prospects is limited and most of the people live in the same area, or where a staff member – the director of development – has an established expertise, knowledge of the constituency, and ability to organize that are likely to be as good as or better than those of anyone brought in to do the job.

The head should work with special-gifts prospects, key leaders, and graduates, help inspire parent soliciting teams, see personally foundation and corporation executives whose organizations may contribute, and generally work wherever the head's influence and personal touch are most needed. Potential major donors almost always expect to see the head of the school.

Relations with governments and associations. In Chapter 3, we speak of the responsibility of the board to keep in touch with what governments are doing and to be aware of their growing influence, which can both strengthen and inhibit independent schools. School heads need to keep an eye out for existing and pending regulations and laws and should, when necessary, alert their boards, some specially designated board member, or the school's legal counsel about new developments. It is helpful, also, for heads to keep in touch with NAIS and other national, regional, and local associations or to delegate this task to a board member or staff member with whom they keep in very close touch. Most school heads these days spend some time consulting with the lawyer or lawyers employed by their schools.

Maintaining good relations between board and head

Why is it that in some schools relations between board and head are characterized by competition, hostility, and working at cross purposes instead of cooperation, mutual support, common goals, and satisfaction in doing an important, difficult job well? Why have some heads been driven from their jobs because of their sense of intolerable frustration or inability to cope? Why have some boards felt they had to take action to fire the head? Why don't some boards and heads, even when they work together over a number of years, get along better and enjoy it more? Here are two main reasons and some suggestions.

First, the difficulty and complexity of the head's job are hard for those not in it to understand. An especially hard part of the job is the pressure from the many groups who feel, in one way or another, that they own the school and know best how to run it: students, parents, teachers, graduates, donors, trustees, and even city, state, and federal governments.

To help heads deal with the difficulties and conflicts inherent in their jobs, the following suggestions for trustees may be useful.

• Encourage close, candid, warm, open relations between head and chairman, where each feels free to express concerns and where one of the chairman's main functions is to support, help, and encourage the head.

• Try not to forget that school heads need praise when they deserve it and are just as hungry as other human beings for approval, hungry to know that others whom they respect appreciate what they are doing, whether it be a speech well delivered, a crisis wisely dealt with, a long-term trial faithfully endured. The nature of their jobs requires heads to appear confident and unruffled. They are seen as powerful people sitting in comfortable offices, one step removed from the daily hurly-burly of the school and with the right to go out to lunch. But never forget it: their life is tough, they work very hard, and they need praise.

• Have a discretionary fund for the head, built into the budget, that allows him or her to solve small problems and to pay for modest but essential activities — sending someone to a conference, taking a trip, buying a piece of equipment, hiring some extra temporary help, inviting someone out to lunch, supporting a small but special school project, getting in a consultant or speaker.

• Encourage the head to mark off on the calendar, well in advance, evenings, and sometimes an entire day, to have time off and say, "I'm sorry, but I'm busy that day." It's amazing and healthy for some heads to see how well their school runs when they are away.

• Make opportunities for heads to meet informally, without

an agenda and in a comfortable place, with a small group of fellow heads, simply for the strength that comes from knowing that they are not alone and for easy sharing of frustrations, information, and good ideas.

• Encourage heads to attend conferences or workshops for fellow heads for sharing, comfort, and stimulation. NAIS can provide information about several such conferences.

A second reason for less than ideal board-head relations is that school heads and trustees sometimes violate the rules of proper distribution of responsibilities. Some heads, for example, try to "get ahead of the interference" by making policy decisions and other important decisions without the advice and consent of the board. They may do this because they feel that, as chief executives and professionals, they are entitled to make decisions on all matters where the board has not specifically reserved the decision to itself. Other heads, who may be somewhat insecure, may bother individual trustees by calling or writing to them about all kinds of minor points, annoying them with routine problems of internal administration that they ought to take care of themselves. At board meetings, they may waste the time of the board by bringing to its attention minor items and requests for permission to do things that are already clearly within the province of the administration.

But heads are not the only culprits. Some trustees—frequently officers or committee chairmen—individually try to dictate to the head, or perhaps tell another administrator what to do. Bad feeling and confusion are bound to result. It is important to point out once again that no individual trustee has authority to give orders or directions to the head or to any member of the faculty or staff. Such authority rests only with the full board in a constituted meeting, and decisions of the board should be communicated to the people concerned through proper channels.

Trustees should always remember that school heads are not subordinates who are given orders, as, for example, the plant manager might be given an order by the president of the company. Although heads are employed by the board, once they are engaged they become the principal person to whom the trustees should look for direction and leadership. As professional educators, they should be expected to lead the board and the school. A clearer analogy is to think of the head of the school as a prime minister. The head is a part of the board in spirit yet stands somewhat apart from it as a leader, and is a leader as long as he or she commands the confidence of the board. When the head loses this confidence and can no longer command the support of a clear working majority of the board, it is time to consider new leadership for the school.

Since the proper relation between making policy and carrying it out is vital to sound relations between boards and heads, let us review it. We have stated that the board makes policy, but we have also stated that heads should be leaders. In that role, it is their responsibility to propose policies, but through proper channels. Experience has shown that the proper avenue of approach to the board with new policies is through the appropriate committee of the board. Therefore, heads who, for example, after consultation and discussion with the faculty, wish to propose a major curriculum change should discuss it first with the trustee committee on education. This committee, which has the time to study educational policy questions in detail, can give the proposal the attention it requires and can then, with the head, report its recommendations to the board. By taking this approach, the head immediately acquires several informed trustees who understand the problem and who can help support the plan, perhaps with revisions jointly arrived at. If the committee turns down the proposal, the head probably will not bring the matter to the board.

Similarly, if the head wishes to improve the overall salary scale of the faculty, this should be discussed thoroughly with the finance committee. Here again, when the proposal is presented to the entire board, the committee will understand the reasons for requesting an improved salary scale and will support the recommendation.

The converse of these procedures is equally true. A valuable channel of communication from the board to the head is the appropriate board committees. These committees have a good opportunity, in a smaller session than a full board meeting, to question the head about the policies and to inform themselves more fully about the operation of the school.

The best way to avoid friction is for board and head to think of themselves, not as competing branches of a single government, but rather as members of a single team. The members of a team have individual functions, but singly they cannot be successful. Only through unity and cooperation under proper leadership can there be success. The head and the trustees should work together, with the trustees acting in their capacity as a board to establish policies and making themselves individually available to the head for help when it is wanted, and the head acting continually as the chief executive officer of the institution, its leader, but always conscious of the head's responsibility to the board and to the board's school constituency.

Reviewing the head's performance

A significant element in promoting and maintaining sound relations between board and head is some sort of regular evaluation in which the head can find out how he or she is doing and at the same time register concerns about the board's performance.

In an NAIS survey of heads in 1979, some, but not all, heads reported some kind of review—usually annual, sometimes at longer intervals—of their performance. It appears, however, that often it was not the kind of candid appraisal we are talking about, but merely an announcement at a board meeting of continuing the head's employment for another year or a note from the treasurer telling of a raise in salary and confirming other benefits for the coming year.

If things are going along all right, one might ask why an evaluation is needed. We believe that school heads, just like teachers, should have the help and reassurance that are provided by a regular review of performance—the review *not* to be tied to discussion of compensation. This is clearly the view of many school heads who do get such a review and many more who do not. One who does not wrote, "I have often felt very lonely in my job, and the lack of any reaction—praise or blame—has made the loneliness more acute. Some periodic review of how the head is doing would certainly be helpful."

Who should do the evaluating? It should be either the chairman of the board or, probably better, the chairman with a few other trustees he or she may wish to involve, but not the full board. We suggest, however, that the chairman ask all members of the board for individual appraisals, if they wish to make them, before the evaluation session so that the chairman may be fully aware of their views.

When and how often should evaluation take place? For most schools and most heads, we suggest once a year. Perhaps the best time is during the summer, when the pressure is less and there is one school year to look back on and another to look forward to. Some heads, however, feel that an evaluation is more realistic and useful if it occurs in the thick of the school year, and they prefer to keep their summers as free as possible from heavy thinking.

In some situations, especially if serious criticism of the head is involved and an informal session or two with the chairman will not suffice, then sessions should probably be more frequent and very specific. Also, for a new head, perhaps periodic evaluation throughout the first year or so is more appropriate; any thoughtful new head will ask for it and board chairman arrange to provide it. For older, experienced heads, an evaluation every two or three years is probably enough. We must also recognize that some heads, teamed with wise trustees, are expert enough at keeping communications open, frank, and constant that no special occasion of evaluation is needed.

It is well for the head to prepare for an evaluation session by writing an informal self-evaluation to be checked against opinions and observations of the trustees responsible for the evaluation. The head may also wish to invite principal administrative associates, and perhaps the faculty, to state their views to the head before the session with the trustee group.

Areas that the evaluators and the head will want to discuss probably include communication with the chairman and the board; maintaining proper balance of responsibilities between board and head; sharing a sense of the mission of the school in a way that moves people to make their best efforts; delegating responsibilities to others but not overdelegating; setting realistic yet challenging objectives; intelligently ordering priorities for accomplishing all that needs to be done; dealing with crises; and explaining to parents and graduates, as well as trustees, changes made or in the making, or changes not being made despite demands for them. These are some main areas to look at. Each school, each year, has its particular list both of concerns and of objectives especially well met and deserving special appreciation. A written summary of the main points of the evaluation, prepared by the chairman for the head, is helpful and provides a benchmark for the next evaluation.

One danger of an evaluation is that the head may be measured against goals and qualities of perfection too high for any person to reach or exemplify. In such a case, an evaluation can be nothing but discouraging. No head can be perfect in all respects. The head who has one particular quality – an always open door with a loving guardian angel just inside to attend to all – may not be the person who can, say, make thoughtful long-range plans and deal wisely with only the problems and crises that no one else can handle. (We should be thankful that the survey turned up only one school that rates its head from 1 to 5 on these criteria: technical knowledge, accomplishment, quality, dependability, acuteness, flexibility, socialness, acceptance, attitude, self-control, initiative, drive, self-confidence, motivation, objectivity, verbal facility, intellectual ability, human relations, leadership, developing others, breadth of knowledge, planning, administration, analysis and judgment, creativeness, capacity, vision, sincerity, sense of humor, resilience, rapport, empathy, fund-raising spark, and "balance between being a 'humanist' and a manager."

An opposite danger is that the evaluation will be a relatively meaningless, time-wasting, bruising or massaging of egos, with no one daring to speak truthfully. It is a mistake to allow an evaluation to consist too heavily either of criticism or of exaggerated praise.

One last point: A close, trusting relationship between the head and the chairman of the board is crucially important. Such a relationship means that the head will receive, both as requested and as needed without having to ask, a steady, constructive evaluation based on commonly understood policies and goals, and that the chairman will receive from the head a similar sort of evaluation of trustees as it is called for and as trustees show themselves needing suggestions, correction, appreciation, praise, or redirection or intensification of energy.

Reviewing the board's performance

What about evaluation of trustees? We have no doubt that the performance of trustees should be evaluated, individually and as a group, but how? And how much time should be given to trustee evaluation?

As mentioned earlier, the nominating committee (committee on trustees) should take an objective look at the quality of service of each trustee annually, but especially when a trustee is up for reappointment. Similarly, individual trustees should evaluate themselves before they agree to serve another term. Early in Chapter 1 we give a list of seven qualifications essential for a trustee. This list can help in trustee evaluation, as can the "Principles of Good Practice for Independent School Trustees" and "Principles of Good Practice for Boards of Trustees of Independent Schools," in Appendix B.

These suggestions may suffice, but NAIS and other groups have evolved more formal and established procedures for trustee evaluation, to assess both their "board work," as a policy-making group, and their "trustee work," as individuals serving the school. Regular board and trustee evaluation can be valuable if it is not overused and if the time consumed in the effort does not drive off the board trustees whose lives are already overfull.

If a board is to evaluate itself, it is important that the evaluation be based on its own corporate objectives for service to the school and on how well it is achieving them. It is also essential, if evaluation is to be done, that the trustees, using a special committee, construct their own instruments for evaluation. One kind of instrument is very simple, allowing members to say whatever is on their minds but not putting ideas in their heads by suggesting problems about which they might not feel fully informed or genuinely concerned. Here is an instrument of this kind used by one school.

Evaluation of the Performance of the
Board of Trustees of The _____ School

Please write anything you think would be helpful about the strengths and weaknesses of the board and note any areas in which you think its service to the school might be improved.

Some areas you may wish to touch on are the composition of the board, its committees, how questions are brought to it, how its meetings are conducted, how well the chairman is performing her functions, the board's service to the school, your own participation in board meetings and committees, your own sense of satisfaction or dissatisfaction with serving on the board, and any other subjects about which you are concerned.

Replies will be read and considered by [name of trustee in charge of the evaluation], who will summarize them in whatever way seems best for making a report. This report will be mailed to you before the meeting on [date], when we will discuss and deal with its suggestions in whatever way we decide. In the report, [name of trustee in charge] may quote directly from some replies, but no names will be used. However, please sign your statement so that she may discuss it with you if she wishes.

The NAIS publication *Evaluating the Performance of Trustees and School Heads* offers a fuller treatment of this subject, along with a number of representative evaluation forms.

How heads can avoid needless friction

We have suggested many ways in which trustees can promote cooperative, productive relations with schools and their heads and help to avoid misunderstanding, conflict, and friction. Let us now consider how school heads, for their part, can avoid actions that arouse the wrath of the trustees or cause them to lose confidence. Even though the head is the chief executive officer and leader, he or she should discuss informally with the chairman of the board, and possibly other senior trustees whose competence or committee membership is particularly relevant, any large anticipated decisions or serious problems that have come up or that loom ahead.

Let us assume, for instance, that a head who is relatively new and young feels it necessary to dismiss a teacher who has been at the school far longer than the head. Technically and legally, the head has the right to hire and fire faculty members and to take action without consulting the board. If this particular head is wise, however, he or she will first discuss this matter with the committee on education, the personnel committee, or the advisory committee, and with the board chairman.

Or suppose that another head feels it necessary to dismiss

the child of a family that has long been associated with the school or the child of a major benefactor. Here again, this head has the right to take this action if deeming it necessary, but would do well to explain this impending action to the chairman of the board and possibly some of the trustees. This does not mean that the head is asking permission, but rather wishes the trustees to understand fully the reasons for this action in case questions come up.

Another way heads can avoid making blunders with board members is to keep close to public opinion. For example, the head may wish to lead the school in a new direction. If conditions are right, the head may be able to do this speedily, but if board and community are not ready for the move or do not understand it, plunging boldly ahead may set back by years the very cause the head espouses. It may take the head a while to prepare the ground and develop support.

It is important, too, for the head to know what students, parents, and others are saying about the school. And the head must stay in constant touch with the faculty to be aware of faculty feelings and morale. Also, any head who is active in community affairs, mingling with parents, trustees, graduates, and others, is better able to anticipate troubles before they become serious. Keeping in touch with opinion is a most important job, so vast in its possibilities for consuming time that many heads deliberately delegate parts of it to members of their staff and to trustees they can count on to inform them if a crisis or other trouble is developing.

In line with these suggestions, the head needs to be receptive to advice. Young, inexperienced heads in particular must avoid trying to assert their own positions by flouting the suggestions of experienced people who already know the territory.

Again, in a spirit of mutual respect and cooperation, the head should always consult with committee chairmen before requesting meetings of committees and should discuss with them the proposed agenda and important topics coming up for discussion. Similarly, the head should discuss with the board chairman the agenda for the board meeting itself, and together they should make the list of topics to be brought up for discussion and decision.

Further, the head can avoid making large errors by paying careful attention to preparation and staff work before any meeting with any group of trustees by being sure to have supporting documents and figures to back up statements. When complex or controversial issues are to come up in a committee meeting, all relevant information should be sent to trustees ahead of time. Even when there is no issue to be decided, it is a good idea for the head to send board committee members memoranda on progress and problems that they should be aware of.

Finally, after any committee or board meeting, it is the responsibility of the head to carry out decisions of the board and to report to the appropriate persons, or to the entire board in some cases, that the decisions have been carried out. The head must judge whether this can be done through a telephone call—to a committee member or officer of the board—or whether the entire board should be informed in writing.

In short, a smoothly working board and smooth board-head relations depend heavily on the thought, imagination, initiative, and hard work of the head.

A contract for the head?

Should the head have a written contract, for a year or longer, with the board? The NAIS survey of school heads in 1979 brought out some interesting facts and some divergent and quite strongly held points of view on this subject. About half the heads had something in writing—a contract or letter of agreement—and about the same number, though not always the same people, favored a contractual arrangement. Often the contract was no more than an undertaking of the board to pay a certain salary, with fringe benefits and perquisites carefully spelled out, and an agreement to those terms by the head.

Many who had no contracts argued against them: "If relationships are sound, contracts are unimportant"; "If trust and respect between head and board go, all the paper in the world is worthless"; and most of this group preferred the informal agreement under which they worked. Many others, however, suggested that contracts would help avoid misunderstanding, that boards change and verbal agreements are forgotten, and so on. And, significantly, many of those who were happy with their no-contract status with their own board said they would favor a contract for their successor, that they would want one if they moved to another school, that they had one when they started but felt it was no longer necessary, or that they favored a contract for the early years of a new head.

Clearly, opinions differ, and it is a matter of mutual agreement between head and board whether or not to formalize the arrangement by a contract or by a letter to the head and signed by the head, which amounts to a contract. Whatever the form of the understanding, there are two objectives to be achieved. One is to set up a working relationship between board and head in which the chance of misunderstanding is minimized. The other, particularly important in these days of shorter tenure for heads, is to regulate the process by which the relationship is terminated so as to avoid damage or unnecessary difficulties to either party.

In the light of all this, we favor having something in writing that (1) spells out in detail the head's salary and perquisites and makes it clear who pays for what in the way of housing, insurance, transportation, school entertaining, and so on, so that there can be no misunderstanding on this score; (2) contains a paragraph or two specifying the duties and responsibilities of the head and those of the board, or refers to the paragraphs in the school's bylaws that deal with them; (3) provides for a periodic review of performance, as discussed above; and (4) specifies the procedures to be followed for renewal — and termination — of the agreement.

Termination of agreement

In most cases, the relationship between a school and its head does not continue until the head retires. Sometimes it does, with great benefit to all, but for all kinds of reasons it usually ends before that. A board may wish to initiate a change; so may a head. Schools at different times in their existence may need different kinds of leadership. The board, or head, or both may sense such a need and decide that a change of leadership is desirable.

Heads may wish to move to other parts of the country, or to different kinds of schools. They may be asked to consider positions involving greater responsibility and opportunity, they may feel they have done all they set out to do at school X and want the challenge of a new set of problems at school Y, or they may simply be tired and seeking a less demanding occupation.

Or differing opinions, strongly held, may develop between board and head on policy questions so basic that neither can accept the other's views about how the school should operate. Assuming frank discussion, good will on each side, and ample notice, it should be possible to resolve these situations amicably and with assurance of a smooth transition.

Other situations exist where the path may not be so smooth and clear. For example, the board has supported the head, working conscientiously with him or her and doing its best to give guidance and direction, but has become increasingly doubtful of the head's eventual success. The new school year is well along, but evidence of incompetence or lack of leadership on the part of the head has become so conspicuous that the board is convinced that there must be a change by the end of the school year. It is too late to give appropriate notice, but the board feels it must ask for the head's resignation and announce the impending change as soon as possible.

Before doing so, the board should ask itself some questions. Has it carefully examined its own actions to assure itself that methods of operation and areas of responsibility have been clearly defined and faithfully adhered to? Has the head been given the authority he or she needs to operate the school within the framework of board policies? And has the board, perhaps out of its concern for the school's welfare, been guilty of interfering in its operations and thus helped to cause a situation that is impossible for the head to deal with? If these questions can be answered satisfactorily, the board should then work with the head to resolve the difficulty. Failing this, the board faces the painful step of making a change in leadership.

Recommended practices. The key factor to be reckoned with in any termination, whether initiated by board or head, is adequate notice. In the interests of the school as well as those of the head, notice should normally be given before a specific date in the year — at least eight to 10 months before the end of a given school year or, better still, a year before. Such extended notice is essential for giving the trustees time to search for and find a successor and for the head to find a new position.

Because notice plays such a critical part in the termination process, it is imperative that equitable financial settlement be provided when appropriate notice cannot be given. In such instances, we recommend continuing the head's salary long enough beyond the school year in which dismissal occurs for the dismissed head to secure acceptable employment. In determining what is "reasonable," consideration should be given to the timing of the dismissal (the later in the school year the greater the obligation), the head's length of service, his or her personal and family circumstances, and the financial condition of the school.

In practice, settlements range from six months to a year. In some cases, agreements call for continuation of salary for a specified number of months or until the head has taken another post. In other cases, agreements provide for a specified period, or amount, of separation pay without condition.

Practices to avoid. A board should not start a search or engage a new head without letting the incumbent know as soon as possible that he or she is on the way out. A search carried on covertly is an affront to the school's constituents as well as to the head.

Heads should not negotiate for a new position in secret, telling their boards they are leaving only after they have found a new job. Individual trustees should not try, on their own initiative, to encourage a head to resign by hinting to him or her that such action would be welcomed by the board.

Dismissal action should be taken by the whole board, not by individuals or committees, and only after the head has been informed of the board's intent, made fully aware of the board's reasons for it, and given ample opportunity to respond. For legal and ethical reasons, the head's right of due process must be respected.

Except for reasons of poor physical or mental health, moral turpitude, or serious dereliction of duty, a head should not be required to leave in the middle of the school year; conversely, a head should not leave in the middle of the year except for a compelling reason of health or family crisis.

Outsiders should not be told of the termination of the head's service before every board member knows, but then they should be informed at the earliest possible moment so that rumor and exaggeration may be stopped by fact. The faculty, parents, students, and the school's public should be informed by a carefully written statement that has been approved by the head and the board.

5.

Selecting a
New Head and
Getting Started

Selecting a new head is probably the most important decision a board of trustees is ever called on to make. It is hard to quarrel with that statement, yet some boards, faced with having to find a new head, handle the task without the care and deliberation its importance dictates, and often with unfortunate results.

The search process

NAIS has a special publication on the search process, *The Selection and Appointment of School Heads.* We recommend that schools seeking a new head consult this manual and that they consider getting in touch with NAIS about other forms of assistance.

The search committee. After the board publicly announces that the present head is leaving or retiring, the selection process begins. The first step is for the board to form a search committee, which should be large enough to represent the views of the major elements of the school community. Trustee members may be joined by one or two graduates or parents. The committee should be small enough to meet frequently and on short notice.

Should faculty members be on the committee? In general, we think that, while it is better not to include them as voting members, faculty opinion should certainly be registered with the search committee, perhaps through one or two faculty representatives. In this way, the faculty acts in an extremely important capacity, for its advice is essential. The faculty should have ample opportunity for its representatives to express faculty convictions about the qualifications desirable in a new head and to register its opinions about specific candidates who are being considered seriously enough to be brought to the school for interviewing.

Having to find a new head gives the board an occasion to take a good look at the school—back five years and forward five years—so that it can share with those candidates who are being seriously considered a realistic and honest statement of the school's mission and condition and of the head's position in its operation. This statement, which can be drafted by a small committee of trustees, possibly with help from the faculty, should be approved by the full board.

Defining the job. At the same time, the search committee should analyze the position of head and write a careful definition of the job and then write a concise description of qualifications and characteristics of the ideal head, knowing that the ideal probably does not exist. Here is a sample checklist for the search committee to keep in mind as it writes its description and considers candidates.

Qualifications	*Characteristics*
Evidence of leadership capacity	Educational philosophy
Academic background	Personality
Teaching experience	Cultural background and interests
Administrative experience	
Public relations experience	
Fund-raising experience	

The search. The committee should plan to allow three to six months for its work. The best season for searching is between Labor Day and March. The committee must be given staff assistance: some secretarial help, an office, a telephone, and a file, possibly away from the school. The committee should include on its list of candidates those already on the school staff who would like to be considered and outsiders. All should be considered equally. It is important that the committee not feel compelled to find someone who lacks the weaknesses of the present head or someone who duplicates the incumbent's strengths. Schools inevitably have to adjust to new heads. They need to regroup and reorganize talents, forces, and arrangements to capitalize on the special talents of the new person.

The NAIS Administrative Clearinghouse Service, other professional placement services, and word of mouth, especially from heads or trustees, are also good sources of names. A number of schools have found their head through advertising in various publications or professional journals or through the suggestion of some interested person who happened to know of a good candidate who was available. The news of a search should be broadcast early and widely. Search committees should not be satisfied merely to sit and examine the records of those who apply or are suggested, however; they should actively search.

Some search committees make good use of consultants, who, though they do not make the selection for the school, can help in defining the job, prescreening candidates, and finding candidates who might match the school's needs. The advantages of appointing a good consultant are great. Consultants can be objective and have extensive experience in analyzing and evaluating resumes and recommendations. Furthermore, they can help direct the search process in an orderly, considerate way, according to a sensible agenda. They help keep the search process balanced; they are not likely to be overinfluenced by superficial charisma or nepotistic connections.

Against these real advantages, however, must be weighed the disadvantages of entrepreneurs in the consulting field. "Head hunters" can be blinded by the seeming importance of the "old boy network," and they may also have their own private criteria for assessing the suitability of a candidate or impose their own agenda on what they think the school needs in a new head. Viewing candidates through these filters may prove discriminatory and limit the selection of candidates.

It is therefore vital for the board and its search committee to remember that consultants work *for* the school and within the school's philosophy, policies, and convictions. No board should abdicate its responsibility to a head hunter. If it does, the match may very well be unfortunate.

Screening. Searching is one thing, screening another. Most good schools could say that the final candidate was chosen from

100, 200, or however many names. The search committee's first step in screening is to go over the resume of each candidate, rejecting those who are obviously not qualified, noting those who look very strong, and placing in a middle category those who look as if they might be good candidates about whom not enough is yet known.

The committee must keep every candidate apprised of his or her status as an applicant. Those who are not to be considered further should be told so politely and promptly; those who look good should be told that their candidacy is being actively considered; and those in the middle should be informed that they are still in the running. Whenever candidates are dropped from consideration, they should be informed at once.

Before any candidate is invited for an interview, references must be checked. The telephone is a convenient and quick way to proceed. Often it brings more forthright evaluations than do written references. Careful notes should be made of all telephone conversations.

Interviewing. Informal preliminary interviews may be held by members of the search committee throughout the selection process and in many locations. There comes a point, however, when some candidates look good enough and seriously interested enough that they should be brought to the school to look at it and be looked at by it. An essential function of the interview is for candidates to see the school as it really is.

The level of candor in interviews must be high. It is foolish to put on any kind of show, because the head, when appointed, will soon know the truth anyway, and the truth is what the head is being employed to deal with. Candidates should be told of any special problems of the school and of any special actions they may be expected to take, such as implementing significant changes in staff or school policy. If a new head is to be given a mandate by the board to make changes disturbing to the established ways or personnel of the school, this mandate should be carefully explained and its implementation discussed in detail. Lack of board and head clarity in such situations is one reason for the disruptive separations that sometimes occur a year or two after a new head is appointed.

Much can be learned about a candidate by asking "What if?" concerning these, and other, situations. What, for example, if applications suddenly fall off generally or in a certain part of the school? What if a generous friend of the school offers the school a facility it doesn't genuinely need? What if a delegation of parents protests against some aspect of the school's program, or one parent makes an angry complaint about a weak teacher? What if a respected long-time faculty member is not competent? What if a group of upper school students rebels and disobeys a major school rule?

Candidates should meet with the chairman of the search committee (or the entire committee), with the chairman of the board, with key members of the school staff, with the outgoing head (unless special reasons make this undesirable), with a group of students, and perhaps with a group of parents and a group of graduates. Candidates should be made welcome to move around the school to get the feel of the place.

As soon as possible after their day of interviews, candidates should be told whether they are still in the running, and, if they are, be asked to say whether they are still interested in the job.

Final selection. When the list of candidates has been narrowed to very few, or when one candidate seems likely to be the strongest, the search committee must make its recommendation to the full board of trustees. If several candidates are involved, the committee can be polled and the candidates ranked. Some committees find it more satisfactory to meet and discuss the finalists in depth until there is agreement on the top candidate and on the ranking of the others. Then the board must meet to hear a full report on the selection process and the recommendation of the search committee, which, except in extraordinary circumstances, should be accepted. The board must meet promptly, because a school cannot afford to keep strong candidates waiting. Usually, other schools are looking at the same candidates at the same time.

As soon as the board confirms the selection, it should be communicated at once, preferably by telephone, to the successful candidate and to the other finalists. Then, also promptly, an announcement to the school's constituency should be made, giving an account of the new head's background and experience. It is wise and considerate, also, to call a special faculty meeting to let the teachers—those most intimately affected—know before the public is informed.

One word of caution: If the deadline the school has set for appointing a new head comes and there is no clear agreement that a strong, right candidate has been found, it is foolish to do what some weary committees do: appoint just anyone to get the job done and the head's office filled. It is much better to take longer to find the right person and to work out the best possible arrangements for carrying on the operations of the school in the meantime. The dangers of a school "spinning its wheels" for a year are almost certainly less than those inherent in an inadequate head.

Under these circumstances, the board should consider the appointment of an interim head for the next academic year. Many schools have a staff member or trustee who knows the school and can keep it going healthily for this period. This person may or may not be a candidate for the head's position; that should be made clear in advance.

Interim heads appointed from without are not uncommon. The appointment of an experienced outsider gives some schools a much-needed breathing space in which to rethink their goals after the departure of a long-tenured, successful head. Under an outside interim head's guidance, necessary changes can sometimes be accepted more readily by board and staff. This grace period may well make the new head's job easier.

In any event, an interim head, either from within or without, should be given full authority to run the school and make all necessary decisions, including staff appointments. The board should resist the temptation to have the school run by a committee.

The head's personal situation

Some selection committees forget that they are usually hiring more than a head. In most cases, whether the candidate is married or single, they are also entering into a relationship with that person's family, whether spouse and children, children from a previous marriage, or aging relatives.

The married head. In many schools, especially when the spouse is a wife, a good deal is expected of her but little is said about it during the selection process. Trustees should take seriously into account the person whose life may be committed at the same time as the new head's and of whom there may be great, unspoken expectations. The spouse of a head should be recognized as an individual, not just as an adjunct. During the interview stage, the candidate's spouse should be interviewed separately, informed what the school's expectations, if any, are, and be given a chance to respond.

The married male candidate may well have a wife who is a professional and expects to continue in her profession. If it happens to be teaching or some aspect of administration or personnel work, she and her husband may both decide to work in the same school—which has advantages and disadvantages. On the other hand, they may prefer not to work in the same place.

Growing numbers of married candidates have spouses whose profession or business is at some distance from the school, which necessitates commuting on weekends or making other plans to be together. The selection committee should explore this situation with the candidate. If it appears that both spouses have made realistic plans for carrying on their respective jobs without disruption to anyone concerned, the committee should not prejudge their ability to do so.

The single head. Whether unmarried, divorced, or widowed, single heads also have particular obligations and needs. As single people, their social needs differ from those of married persons. It may, for example, be especially important for them to belong to certain clubs or organizations and to have individual trustees take an active personal interest in introducing them to the school community and beyond. Further, it should be recognized that single heads in particular, though not exclusively, may need housekeeping arrangements that will enable them to function more freely as heads and in whatever social role has been mutually agreed upon.

Entertaining. It is important that the school's expectations for "entertaining" be specifically discussed. Most heads (and their spouses) are expected to act as friendly hosts, but the school should not assume either that they will cook and serve or that they will even wish to supervise others performing these duties. Some heads make it clear that social entertaining for school purposes is not their forte or pleasure and that they expect others to perform this function. While the ability to entertain is an asset, and may in some schools be deemed essential, it should not be tacitly assumed.

A final note. The selection committee should be prepared to explore with and articulate to candidates any expectations the school has in the area of personal and social values, including a clear statement of the extent to which the school and its trustees can tolerate and support variations from these expectations. Here is an area where candor and thoroughness early on can help avoid misunderstanding and friction later, when it is sometimes too late to deal with these constructively.

After the new head takes charge

Some special attention must now be given to something that is of almost equal importance to that of selecting a new head: ensuring the success of the new administration and giving it strength and support. It is perhaps not too far-fetched to compare a school and its new head to a newly married couple. If the marriage is to work, each must be ready to adjust to the other—to get used to the other's ways, and to recognize and be ready to help avoid or overcome difficulties that are apt to arise—until full understandings are reached and the partnership can be considered a success. Some schools have found that two or three members of the search committee, who may have come to know the head, or one or two other trustees, can take responsibility for this important function.

The start of a new administration can be a touchy period, and it can take as much as two years for faculty, parents, and students to get over the change. It would be surprising, and unusual, if no group regretted the departure of the former head and was not uncomfortable, or at least not convinced, about the new one. Here are some suggestions to trustees about helping a new head in the first two years.

• The board should be sure that the former head, if he or she remains in the community, does not continue as a member of the board.

• The board chairman should be especially alert to proper handling of complaints by trustees (as covered near the end of Chapter 3). Above all, the board chairman should make the new head feel that the chairman is a friend who wants to make the new administration a success, one who will support the head through a period of considerable stress. It is almost inevitable that a few parents and teachers will find things to complain about in a new administration, if only because it is not just like the old one. If the board makes it clear that the new head has its confidence and backing, the situation will almost certainly right itself soon enough.

• The new head must make an equal effort to keep the lines of communication open, talking over any difficulties that arise and that the board chairman may not know about, and not trying to conceal them in the hope that they will not come to the attention of the board.

• When a new head has been charged with making changes in personnel or methods of operation, it may be useful for the chair, or another trustee or two, to help the head devise strategies to negotiate these difficulties and to deal with the perceptions of the community. Whoever performs the functions suggested above must, however, be careful not to become, or seem to become, a special channel to the head.

What about the outgoing head?

The former head, if remaining in the community of the school, should be very careful to stay entirely out of the affairs of the school and especially to avoid getting involved in any discussions of dissatisfaction or resentment of change. The former head should understand, as should the former head's friends and family, that it is the new head's show.

In some situations, former heads have continued to be very useful to their schools, and new heads have strongly encouraged them in this. Probably no one knows the school, its problems, its strengths, its people, and its politics better than the outgoing head. It seems a shame not to make use of this knowledge. However, most outgoing heads are more than happy to give over the reins of power, with its pressures and responsibilities. They are entirely ready for a new life and have not the slightest desire to run anything as strenuous as a school or being even peripherally involved in its tangles.

Further, in most cases, no one understands better than a former school head the trials and complications that ensue when any person intrudes on the responsibility of a school head. This being the case, the former head can, without harm and with great benefit, be available to the new head, advising when asked and, at the same time, giving unqualified support to the new administration. The former head does not interfere, is not on the board, is not open to complaints, but is an asset and strength.

Several schools have made even more intensive use of their former heads. For example, some retired heads have successfully directed or helped in capital gifts and deferred giving campaigns, some have traveled around the country to meet with groups of graduates and large donors, past and prospective. The former head can also serve by reassuring the constituency that the school is in good hands and that its mission is as important as ever.

Whatever relations between schools and their retired heads may be, the question is one that deserves the most careful thought by the new head, the old head, and the board.

6.

A Postscript

Trustees are considered by many people, otherwise intelligent, to be a strange species: rich, stingy, blind, leisured, and full of notions. Mark Twain once said that school boards were "what God made, after he practiced making idiots."

Fortunately, Twain also said, "Truth is a rare commodity, and therefore should be used sparingly." In our experience, the truth is, and should be expressed unsparingly, that trustees are for the most part hard-working, conscientious, intelligent men and women. Independent schools could not have gotten to where they are today without them.

The fact that this handbook has been revised four times since its original publication in 1964 testifies to the steady evolution of the role and responsibility of the independent school trustee. At the same time, we have seen no reason to change in any significant way the statement of fundamental principles made in the first edition.

However, no alert trustee of any independent school needs to be reminded of the many new issues schools face: how to finance independent education; changing relations among trustees, administrators, teachers, and students; new philosophies about teaching methods and what is to be taught; pressure from governments to regulate—to be resisted when regulation is likely to stultify, to be accepted when it promises to serve justice and democracy; the increasing need for legal counsel to help deal creatively with the requirements of law and threats from those who use it to work against the schools; and the independent school's relation to public education, which it must help to support and strengthen.

Abundant credit must be given to boards and school heads for not merely breasting tides that once seemed capable of overwhelming them but for moving their schools forward. And while relations between board and head are not invariably perfect, most heads have rewarding relationships with their boards and find their members thoroughly loyal and helpful.

There have always been some who predicted the end of independent schools, but their predictions have always proved wrong. In general, enrollment in independent schools is increasing, even while the school population as a whole is declining. The schools are a vigorous, varied, and vital part of the social machinery of American democracy.

It is clear that to be a trustee of an independent school is not an honorary position or a sinecure. As all trustees worthy of the name know, trusteeship calls for hard work and intelligent judgment on many difficult and challenging issues affecting many people. The rewards of trusteeship, and they are great, lie primarily in the inner satisfaction that comes from being part of an essential and often noble enterprise. Those who really understand the sources of strength of independent schools should be grateful to trustees for being one of the most important of those sources.

Appendix A

NAIS Publications

The following publications, of interest to trustees, may be ordered from the National Association of Independent Schools, 18 Tremont Street, Boston, Massachusetts 02108; tel. (617) 723-6900. Current prices are available upon request.

Books

Evaluating the Performance of Trustees and School Heads, by Eric W. Johnson. As another bridge to effective board-head relations, this manual presents evaluation as a means to strengthen the school and everyone in it by encouraging people and showing them how they might perform at their best. 1983.

Faculty Salary Systems in Independent Schools, by John C. Littleford and Valerie Lee. This research report gives detailed case studies and commentary on faculty salary systems in nine NAIS member schools chosen for their diversity of approach and strong commitment to high faculty salaries. 1983.

How the Board Can Promote Faculty Effectiveness, by Milbrey W. McLaughlin. This essay tells how trustees can and should go beyond issues of mere job satisfaction among faculty members and, instead, provide support for professionalism. 1984.

Independent School Effectiveness: A New Emphasis, by Thomas Read. This summary of recent research on school effectiveness offers an extensive bibliography. 1983.

A Legal Primer for Independent Schools, by Albrecht Saalfield. This primer offers general background reading to heighten awareness of the possible consequences of action and inaction in various areas of school life. It serves to illustrate the ideals and standards by which a good independent school is operated. 1983.

Long-Range Planning for Independent Schools. Detailed description of the planning and policy development process formulated by the Commission on Educational Issues to help schools consider educational and financial alternatives. 1979.

Principles of Good Practice for Independent School Trustees. This 11-part statement outlines the obligations and responsibilities of independent school trustees to the school and to the board. 1984. Reproduced in Appendix B, below.

Principles of Good Practice for Boards of Trustees of Independent Schools. This 13-part statement outlines the duties and responsibilities of the board of trustees to the school and in its own functioning. 1984. Reproduced in Appendix B, below.

School Loan Program Guide. Loans, becoming a customary form of financial aid among elementary and secondary schools, enable a school to extend and renew its financial aid resources. The guide gives a concise overview of financial aid and the role of loans and explores some of the questions that most often arise in connection with loans. 1984.

The Selection and Appointment of School Heads, by Eileen R. Driscoll. If the board of trustees performs the task of finding a new head carefully and well, all parties concerned—and especially the school—will benefit. This manual addresses issues and questions that arise as the school moves into new leadership. Sections addressed to boards and candidates are followed by seven appendixes outlining procedures and questions involved in the search and appointment process. 3rd ed., 1982.

Teaching School: Points Picked Up, by Eric W. Johnson. An overview of teaching as it relates to teachers, students, school, and community, with order, interest, spirit, and discipline serving as cornerstones. 1979; revised 1981.

Periodicals

Independent School. The quarterly journal of NAIS, containing feature articles, NAIS Reporter (with special news of NAIS, member schools, other programs), and book reviews.

NAIS Statistics. Surveys of tuition fees, salaries, enrollments, and other data. Published in two parts, fall and winter. Available to members only.

NAIS Publications. Special combination subscription for administrators and trustees (members only): *Independent School, Administrative Forum*, annual report, legislative memoranda, conference announcements, and other materials.

Workshops

Each year various association programs are available for trustees; some are sponsored locally, others are initiated by NAIS. In addition, the annual Workshop for Board Chairmen is offered for board chairmen who wish to learn more about independent school trusteeship.

Appendix B

Principles of Good Practice

The following sets of principles of good practice for independent school trustees are addressed, respectively, to trustees as individuals and to trustees acting in concert as a board.

Principles of Good Practice for Independent School Trustees

The responsibility of a trustee of an independent school is to gain a basic understanding of all aspects of the school's operations and then to initiate, or support, board actions that will advance the standards and goals set forth in the school's statement of philosophy. The following Principles of Good Practice for Independent School Trustees are offered to encourage the full participation of every trustee in the important work of the board. They are endorsed by the NAIS Board of Directors, the Trustee Committee, the School Heads Advisory Committee, and NAIS management.

1. A trustee's first obligation is to become informed about the school's history, goals, and current operations and concerns.

2. A trustee should come to meetings prepared, having read the minutes of previous meetings and other pertinent materials, and should participate in the consideration of all matters before the board. Only through the sharing of diverse opinions can constructive decisions be reached.

3. A trustee should not hesitate to ask questions. A full understanding of the issues is prerequisite to casting an informed vote.

4. A board of trustees, as a whole, sets policy. An individual trustee should never seek to impose a personal agenda on the head of the school or become involved in specific management or curricular issues.

5. A trustee must always respect the confidentiality of board discussions. The credibility of the board goes hand in hand with confidentiality.

6. Trustees should seek out and volunteer for assignments, particularly those that may lessen the special burdens carried by the head, such as serving as the school's representative at conferences and meetings.

7. A trustee must guard against any conflict of interest, whether business-related or personal. Trustees who are parents must take particular care to separate the interests of the school from those of a child.

8. A trustee has a responsibility to support the school head actively and to demonstrate that support within the school community.

9. The trustee who learns of a problem should bring that problem to the attention of the school head or board president. A trustee should not attempt to deal with such situations on an individual basis.

10. Every trustee has a responsibility to contribute to the advancement program of the school. This should include, but not be limited to, financial support or other active involvement in annual giving and capital campaigns as an integral part of trusteeship.

11. Each trustee, not just the treasurer or finance committee, has a fiduciary responsibility for the funds entrusted to the school and for sound budgetary management.

Principles of Good Practice for Boards of Trustees of Independent Schools

In an independent school, the responsibility of the board of trustees is to be aware, to the fullest extent possible, of all matters that pertain to the philosophy and goals of the school and to assure that decisions of the board conform to these stated objectives. The following Principles of Good Practice for Boards of Trustees are set forth to provide a common perspective of the board's responsibilities for individual trustees, board presidents, and school heads. They are endorsed by the NAIS Board of Directors, the Trustee Committee, the School Heads Advisory Committee, and NAIS management.

1. The board is responsible for preparing a clear statement of the school's philosophy and objectives. This philosophy should be reviewed on a regular basis and taken into consideration whenever possible changes of policy are under discussion.

2. The board has complete and final responsibility in all fiscal affairs of the school including assets represented by buildings and grounds.

3. The board is responsible for selecting a new head of the school, when needed. Care should be exercised against delegating too great a responsibility in this most critical matter to nonboard persons or consultants.

4. The board is responsible for establishing the policies under which the head will administer the school. Every school should include in its catalogue a policy statement regarding non-discrimination and reflect this policy in its faculty, staff, and student mix.

5. The board must ensure that the school has sufficient public relations capacity, under competent leadership, to convey the school's message to the public and to the school's various constituencies.

6. The board should establish working committees and be sure that all members are actively involved in appropriate committee assignments.

7. The board is responsible for a periodic evaluation of the school, taking into consideration the school's stated philosophy and goals. Board members should be given copies of any periodic evaluations conducted by outside accrediting organizations.

8. The board, or a committee of the board, should conduct a written annual evaluation of the performance of the head and establish goals for the following year. Because this review should not relate to compensation, it should be undertaken only after the matter of compensation has been settled.

9. The board should conduct a written annual self-evaluation, including consideration of whether the board and its committees are independently knowledgeable concerning school matters or are relying too heavily upon the head and other staff for guidance. The head of the school should also evaluate the board's performance.

10. The board is responsible for keeping full and accurate minutes of its meetings and those of its committees.

11. The board should maintain a policy book so that governing decisions made over a period of years may be readily available to subsequent leadership and administrators.

12. A rotation system for board membership should be established to assure regular infusion of new thinking while maintaining continuity of volunteer leadership to work with the head of the school. The composition of the board should reflect whatever diversity exists among the school's constituencies. It may be necessary for the board actively to recruit members from other groups to achieve this diversity.

13. The board should establish a policy of sharing statistical information about the school with local and national professional organizations.